Fifty More
Professional Scenes
and Scenes
Monologs *for*
Student
Actors

A collection of short one- and two-person scenes

Garry Michael Kluger

mp
MERIWETHER PUBLISHING LTD.
Colorado Springs, Colorado

Meriwether Publishing Ltd., Publisher
PO Box 7710
Colorado Springs, CO 80933-7710

Editor: Ted Zapel
Cover design: Jan Melvin

© Copyright MMIV Meriwether Publishing Ltd.
Printed in the United States of America
First Edition

Library of Congress Cataloging-in-Publication Data

Kluger, Garry Michael,
  Fifty more professional scenes and monologs for student actors : a collection of short one- and two-person scenes / Garry Michael Kluger.--1st ed.
      p. cm.
  ISBN 1-56608-095-9
1. Dialogues. 2. Monologues. 3. Acting. I. Title.
  PN2080.K63 2004
  792.02'8--dc22

                                    2004006482

        1   2   3   4   04   05   06

*To my wife Lori, my daughter Emily, and my son Noah —
my family. They give me all the love and happiness I could
ask for and enough surprises to make life continually
worth writing about. I love them with all my heart.*

*And finally, this book is dedicated to actors everywhere.
Just remember to enjoy what you're doing, for the joy in
acting comes from the creating.*

Contents

Foreword 1

Introduction 3

Section One
Comedy 5

  1. Blind Faith 7

  2. An Acting Experience 11

  3. An Acting Experience II 15

  4. Mother 19

  5. The Casting Session 22

  6. The Ghost 26

  7. The Funeral 30

  8. The Collector 34

  9. The Lawsuit 38

  10. The Drawing Room 42

  11. The Conference 46

  12. The Morning After 50

  13. The Plan 54

  14. The Stakeout 58

  15. The Ballplayer 61

  16. The Will 64

  17. The Tutor 68

  18. The Sister 72

  19. The Withdrawal 76

  20. Students 81

Section Two
Drama 85

  21. The Confrontation 87

  22. The Diagnosis 90

  23. The Meeting 94

  24. The Sponsor 97

  25. The Affair 101

26. The Patsy 105
27. The Last Good-bye 109
28. Loss 113
29. The Split 117
30. Good-bye 121
31. The New Boss 124
32. The Old Friend 129
33. The Settlement 133
34. The Session 138
35. The Strangers 143
36. The Testimony 146
37. The Caseworker 150
38. The Decision 154
39. The Tenant 158
40. The Escort 162

Section Three
Multi-Person 167
41. The Commercial 169
42. Next 172

Section Four
Monologs 177
43. Mickey 179
44. Heartache 181
45. Dating 183
46. The Fifties I 185
47. New Year's Eve 186
48. The Fifties II 188
49. After a Year 189
50. The Rock Star 190

About the Author 193

Foreword

"Can you please come back in and do a scene of your choice?" These can be the most exciting words an actor can hear — and the most terrifying. Choosing a scene to showcase your talents can be a daunting task — so many books, so many choices! My advice to other actors has always been to find contemporary, age-appropriate material for auditions. (Trust me — no one wants to see a twenty-one-year-old play Uncle Vanya no matter how great they thought you were in your high school production!) The really difficult task is to find a scene they haven't heard (the orgasm scene from *When Harry Met Sally* is so funny — the first *fifty* times). For me, the choice was always easy — I would call my good friend Garry Kluger and ask to look through his latest offerings. Garry's scenes are always fresh, funny, and can be used for auditioning for the stage, screen, and television. They are also really good for use in acting class. So, take your time going through the following pages — I'm confident you will find the perfect scene. It has always worked for me. Performing one of Garry's scenes (it's called "The Plan" and it's in this book) secured me my first "real" agent in Los Angeles. I am eternally grateful to Garry for his wonderful work — and you will be too!

Break a leg!

Heather Paige Kent

Heather Paige Kent starred in the CBS series *That's Life* and the NBC series *Stark Raving Mad* and *Jenny*.

Introduction

The scenes included in this book have been written over several years and many have been filmed by over 250 actresses and actors. They have also been performed in theatres, classes, showcases, and have been used by major networks to audition actors from coast to coast. In other words, people seem to like them. I guess if they didn't, this wouldn't be my third book of scenes.

I am writing this introduction because I want the actors and actresses who use this material to be aware of a couple of things. A great number of the scenes in this book are, for the most part, gender non-specific. Meaning that they can be performed in any combination of actor and actress desired. The dialog appears in a specific form. Instead of a line like, "He went to the store" or "She went to the store," what you would see is "He/She went to the store." The pronoun used would depend on who is being spoken about. The same applies to a line like "My husband is great" or "My wife is great." It would appear as "My husband/wife is great." Then it would depend on who is speaking.

On another note there is one scene in the book: "The Last Good-Bye." It was more or less a commissioned scene, and it's in a very specific style. Once you read it you will see that it is very 1940s type in its setting and dialog. I included it in the book because I thought some of you might have a lot of fun with this scene, especially if you want to try a period piece.

And lastly — I have been a writer for a long time and an actor even longer, and what I've found is that no matter what the scene, drama or comedy, you have to enjoy the experience. These scenes can be sad, funny, poignant, and dramatic, but they should always be *fun* to perform. Please get all the excitement out of these scenes that you can while you perform them. See — if you don't enjoy what you're doing, how can the audience? Enjoy!

Garry Kluger

P.S. I'd love to hear any comments or stories you might have about these scenes. You can leave me a message at iktproductions@sbcglobal.net

Section One
Comedy

1. Blind Faith

CAST: MALCOLM, FAITH

SCENE OPENS: We are at a dance. Seated on the opposite sides of the stage are MALCOLM and FAITH. The two are young, early twenties and could still be in college. MALCOLM keeps looking over at FAITH. She seems to be looking at him also. MALCOLM prepares himself, then screws up his courage and goes over to her.

MALCOLM: Excuse me.

FAITH: Yes?

MALCOLM: Well, I usually don't do this, but I was sitting over there and I noticed you were looking at me, and ... I was looking at you, so I thought that I would come over and introduce myself.

FAITH: I was looking at you?

MALCOLM: I hope so, otherwise I just made a gigantic jackass out of myself. And you know what — never mind. I'll be leaving now and, well, drowning myself in the punch bowl. It's been nice talking to you. 'Bye. *(He starts to exit.)*

FAITH: Wait, you didn't give me a chance to say anything.

MALCOLM: You mean you were looking at me?

FAITH: Well, not exactly, but I'm glad you thought so.

MALCOLM: Why?

FAITH: If you hadn't then you would have never come over.

MALCOLM: Thank you. *(Pause)* I think. My name is Malcolm.

FAITH: Mine's Faith.

MALCOLM: Nice to meet you. *(He sits next to her.)* So, having a good time?

FAITH: In a word, no!

MALCOLM: Really, you too? I hate these dances.

FAITH: Then why did *you* come?

MALCOLM: My friends dragged me along.

FAITH: Mine, too. My girlfriends said I don't get out enough. They promised me I'd have a good time. *(Pause)* They lied.

1   MALCOLM: As long as we're both having such a lousy time, why
2   don't we have it together? Let's dance.
3   FAITH: I don't think so.
4   MALCOLM: Why not?
5   FAITH: I'm not very good at it.
6   MALCOLM: Perfect, neither am I. Let's stink together. *(He takes*
7   *her by the hand and on to the floor. They start to dance. The two*
8   *are rather tentative and clumsy.)*
9   MALCOLM: You know what?
10   FAITH: What?
11   MALCOLM: You were right. You're not very good. I'm much
12   worse, of course, but just the same ... *(The two pause, and then*
13   *both start to laugh.)*
14   MALCOLM: Well, why don't we sit down before we embarrass
15   ourselves further?
16   FAITH: Good idea. *(MALCOLM sits. FAITH stands there for a*
17   *moment. She reaches out for a chair.)*
18   MALCOLM: Why don't you sit down?
19   FAITH: Is there another chair here? *(MALCOLM indicates a chair*
20   *nearby.)*
21   MALCOLM: Yeah, right over there.
22   FAITH: Where?
23   MALCOLM: Right over there, can't you see it?
24   FAITH: Well, *(Pause)* no.
25   MALCOLM: What do you mean, no?
26   FAITH: I mean I can't see it. I'm blind.
27   MALCOLM: What do mean you're blind? You mean like you can't
28   see?
29   FAITH: You know another definition of blind? *(There is no*
30   *response.)* Could you do me a favor while you're coming out of
31   shock and get me a chair?
32   MALCOLM: I'm sorry. *(He runs over and gets the other chair. He*
33   *brings it over and helps her into it.)* Here, let me help you.
34   FAITH: That's OK, I've been seating myself since I was twelve.
35   *(She waits for a response and gets none.)* Laugh — that was a

1   joke. *(MALCOLM waves his hand in front of FAITH's face.)*

2   FAITH: Please don't do that.

3   MALCOLM: How did you know what I was doing?

4   FAITH: Malcolm, I'm blind, not stupid. I can feel and hear what

5   you're doing.

6   MALCOLM: Sorry.

7   FAITH: It's OK, everybody does it.

8   MALCOLM: Well, ... um ... nice dance, huh?

9   FAITH: Oh boy, here it comes.

10   MALCOLM: Here what comes?

11   FAITH: The perfunctory small talk. "How do you like school?

12   What are you studying? You know, you're my first blind

13   person." Things like that.

14   MALCOLM: Well — what *are* you studying?

15   FAITH: *(Pause)* Photography, all right?

16   MALCOLM: Hey, you wanna cut me a break? I don't do that well

17   with sighted girls. You're a whole new challenge.

18   FAITH: I'm sorry. I thought you knew about me.

19   MALCOLM: How would I know about you?

20   FAITH: You're in Hoffman's history class.

21   MALCOLM: Yeah, how did you know?

22   FAITH: I know your voice. You sit behind me.

23   MALCOLM: That's pretty incredible.

24   FAITH: Not really. Wouldn't you recognize your friend's voices

25   even if you couldn't see them?

26   MALCOLM: Yes, I suppose so.

27   FAITH: Do you consider it that big a feat?

28   MALCOLM: No.

29   FAITH: See?

30   MALCOLM: I guess so. I never thought of it that way. I am sorry if

31   I acted strangely. I just never tried to pick up a blind girl before.

32   FAITH: Then just pretend I'm sighted.

33   MALCOLM: That wouldn't work.

34   FAITH: Why?

35   MALCOLM: 'Cause I usually strike out with them too.

1   FAITH: How come? You seem like a nice guy.
2   MALCOLM: Well, girls today all seem to go for the guys who look
3   like rock stars.
4   FAITH: *I* don't know what any rock stars look like.
5   MALCOLM: In that case I look just like most of them.
6   FAITH: It wouldn't matter. I've heard you in class and around,
7   and I've kinda wanted to meet you.
8   MALCOLM: Why didn't you just introduce yourself?
9   FAITH: For obvious reasons. I'm afraid I don't make friends that
10   easily.
11   MALCOLM: I guess I can understand.
12   FAITH: Can you?
13   MALCOLM: I don't make friends all that easily either.
14   FAITH: From listening to you I thought you would.
15   MALCOLM: Well, I … you don't want to hear all this.
16   FAITH: Sure I do.
17   MALCOLM: Really?
18   FAITH: Yeah.
19   MALCOLM: Well then, why don't we get out of here and go some
20   place quiet?
21   FAITH: That sounds good. *(They both stand up.)*
22   MALCOLM: Now what do I do?
23   FAITH: What do you do!? Am I going to have to talk you through —
24   *everything*? This could be a long night.
25   MALCOLM: I mean, do you need any help now? *(FAITH starts to*
26   *laugh.)*
27   FAITH: Here, let me take your arm. *(She takes ahold.)* **Ready?**
28   MALCOLM: Yeah, let's go. *(They start to leave and MALCOLM trips*
29   *over FAITH's purse, pulling them both down. They start to laugh.)*
30   Here, I think you forgot your purse.
31   FAITH: Thanks, maybe I should lead. *(They both laugh again.*
32   *Lights out.)*
33   **The End**
34
35

2. An Acting Experience

CAST: ADAM, JILLIAN

SCENE OPENS: We are in a living room. ADAM is seated on the couch reading the paper. JILLIAN enters, just back from an audition. She stands at the end of the couch, very tightlipped, obviously very angry and staring at ADAM. He looks up.

ADAM: Hi. *(JILLIAN, without saying a word, looks at him, takes her bag from her shoulder, sets it on the floor, then kicks it across the room. She then throws her script down on the floor and screams a very frustrated scream — very loudly! ADAM waits until she's done.)* **I take it the audition didn't go very well.**

JILLIAN: *Go to hell!*

ADAM: Ah — that good. *(JILLIAN starts to pace.)*

JILLIAN: What does he know anyway?

ADAM: Who?

JILLIAN: Who do you think? If I ever see that little putz again I'm going to rip his ... He'll wish he never heard my name ... He'll ...

ADAM: OK, OK. Calm down ...

JILLIAN: But he ...

ADAM: But he nothing. *Sit!* *(She does.)* **Good. Now, tell me what happened.**

JILLIAN: Well. I went into this office and I was introduced to this — slug who calls himself a director. He told me I wasn't right for the part and he wouldn't let me read.

ADAM: Why?

JILLIAN: I don't know.

ADAM: OK — let me see the script and maybe we can both figure it out.

JILLIAN: Fine. *(She gets up, grabs her bag, pulls a crumpled ball of papers out and hands it to ADAM. She then sits next to him.)*

ADAM: What were you reading for?

JILLIAN: Mary. She comes in on page seventeen.

1   **ADAM:** Mary?

2   **JILLIAN:** *Mary!*

3   **ADAM:** Mary. *(He skims the script, stops, looks at JILLIAN, then*

4   *proceeds to read aloud.)* "Mary enters. She is a young pretty

5   girl. She is approximately seventeen years old — and black."

6   Did your agent send you in on this?

7   **JILLIAN:** No — Judy Lloyd read for it and she told me about it.

8   **ADAM:** Judy Lloyd is black.

9   **JILLIAN:** It doesn't matter. I'm a better actress than she is.

10   **ADAM:** But she's black!

11   **JILLIAN:** I don't care! I can play that part. I've been to

12   Strasberg's; I've been to the Actor's Studio. *(Proudly)* I can

13   run naked on stage!

14   **ADAM:** And I suppose you told him that.

15   **JILLIAN:** Of course!

16   **ADAM:** Of course. Jilly, I think you're missing the point here —

17   **JILLIAN:** *(Cutting him off)* Wait a minute. Do you think he treated

18   me fairly? Would you have done that to me?

19   **ADAM:** Me — no. I would have had you committed.

20   **JILLIAN:** *(Indignant)* Why?

21   **ADAM:** Because you're crazy, that's why.

22   **JILLIAN:** I should have known better than to talk to you. You have

23   no sensitivity or understanding.

24   **ADAM:** I have no sensitivity or understanding?

25   **JILLIAN:** You got it, Ace!

26   **ADAM:** You want to know what it's like living with you and your

27   career? No, don't answer. I'll tell you. It's like living with

28   Sybil. Do you know that in the last week I have made love with

29   Lady Macbeth, Joan of Arc, and Blanche Dubois? *(JILLIAN*

30   *starts to jump in, but ADAM stops her.)* OK, I'll give you that

31   Blanche was fun — but last night was the limit.

32   **JILLIAN:** Why? I thought it would be exciting.

33   **ADAM:** Jillian — I didn't want to sleep with King Lear.

34   **JILLIAN:** Why not?! He's royalty. He's got charm, he's got

35   charisma, he's got —

1   ADAM: He's got a beard! You're making me question my own
2   sexuality here. You're ... I don't know why I'm talking about
3   this. I don't have a problem. You do! You are not going to
4   work until you change your approach.
5   JILLIAN: How?
6   ADAM: Start telling the truth!
7   JILLIAN: *(Pause)* What?
8   ADAM: Start being honest about yourself.
9   JILLIAN: Honest? With casting people? Are you crazy? No way!
10   ADAM: Why not?
11   JILLIAN: Because I've never done that before. I don't even think
12   I know how.
13   ADAM: Then don't think of it as being honest. Think of it as an ...
14   acting exercise.
15   JILLIAN: An acting exercise?
16   ADAM: Yeah, *(Searching)* yeah, uh ... you know. You know how
17   you are when you're not thinking about the business?
18   JILLIAN: No.
19   ADAM: No — OK, uh, you know how you were when we went to
20   Tijuana?
21   JILLIAN: No — yes!
22   ADAM: Well, that's Jillian Carson, real person. Be her. Act like
23   her the next time you have an audition.
24   JILLIAN: Jillian Carson, real person, huh? *(Thinking)* You know,
25   that's crazy enough to work. She's an easy character. Hell, I
26   could probably do her in my sleep.
27   ADAM: That certainly would be a switch.
28   JILLIAN: *(Getting excited)* Yeah, it'll work! That's a great idea.
29   Why didn't I think of it? Thank you, honey. *(ADAM goes back
30   to work. JILLIAN picks up a* Variety *and starts practicing her new
31   approach.)* Hi, I'm Jillian Carson, real person, and I want to
32   give you my picture and resume. No. Hi, I'd like to ... *(She
33   notices something in the paper.)* Oh my God!!
34   ADAM: What?
35   JILLIAN: They're auditioning "Boy in the Band." I'm perfect for

1   **the lead.** *(ADAM gets up and leaves the room, followed by*
2   *JILLIAN who keeps talking.)* **No, Adam, really. I can play gay.**
3   **All I need is a little moustache ...**
4   **The End**
5
6
7
8
9
10
11
12
13
14
15
16
17
18
19
20
21
22
23
24
25
26
27
28
29
30
31
32
33
34
35

3. An Acting Experience II

CAST: ADAM, JILLIAN

SCENE OPENS: We are in the living room of ADAM CRAIG. He is a writer. He enters the room. He puts his things down and starts to pace. He also starts to practice a speech of some kind.

ADAM: **Jilly, honey, you know, life's funny sometimes ... No she'll never buy that. OK, how about ... Jilly, you want to hear something funny? ... God, What am I going to do?** *(Just then we hear JILLIAN Off-stage.)*

JILLIAN: **Adam, are you home?** *(JILLIAN CARSON enters. She is ADAM's girlfriend. She is an actress. She has just come back from the auditions for ADAM's first play. She is very excited. ADAM tries to sneak out of the room. JILLIAN stops him.)* **Adam, hi. Why didn't you answer me?**

ADAM: **Oh — sorry, didn't hear you. And I was about to go take care of that ... thing you wanted me to take care of.**

JILLIAN: **What thing?**

ADAM: **The thing, thing.**

JILLIAN: **Oh — that thing? Well, that can wait. So, tell me. How did the rest of the auditions go, Mr. Playwright?**

ADAM: **Fine, just fine.** *(He sits on the couch. She plops down next to him, very excited.)*

JILLIAN: **It was so exciting to audition on a stage and know that the playwright sitting out there is your boyfriend, the one you love more than anyone in the world. The one who loves you the same way.** *(ADAM stares at her, then looks away and starts to talk to himself under his breath.)*

ADAM: *(Under his breath)* **Please — someone just kill me now.**

JILLIAN: **What?**

ADAM: **Nothing. I just said you were right.**

JILLIAN: **Oh, anyway, were you proud of me?**

ADAM: **Yes, I was.**

JILLIAN: **What did you think of my audition?**

1   **ADAM:** You know I can't talk about that.

2   **JILLIAN:** Why not?

3   **ADAM:** 'Cause it wouldn't be fair to all the others who auditioned.

4   *(JILLIAN starts to kiss his ear and neck and face.)*

5   **JILLIAN:** Come on, baby, tell your Jilly what you thought. *(ADAM*

6   *starts to close his eyes and get into this, then remembers. He*

7   *jumps up.)*

8   **ADAM:** OK, um ... I thought ... you ... were ... Boy, was I proud

9   of you.

10   **JILLIAN:** You've said that.

11   **ADAM:** I did? I did. Sorry. What was the question?

12   **JILLIAN:** Never mind. I guess it isn't fair to put you on the spot.

13   **ADAM:** Thank you. *(He heaves a sigh.)*

14   **JILLIAN:** Just tell me when the callbacks are.

15   **ADAM:** The what?

16   **JILLIAN:** The callbacks? You know, the auditions after the first

17   ones.

18   **ADAM:** I know what callbacks are.

19   **JILLIAN:** Good, when are they?

20   **ADAM:** Uh ... Friday.

21   **JILLIAN:** What time is mine?

22   **ADAM:** *(Under his breath)* God, here it comes. *(To her)* Jilly, you

23   don't have to come back. *(She screams and jumps off the couch.)*

24   **JILLIAN:** *I got the part! (She runs over to him, throws her arms*

25   *around him, and starts to kiss him.)* Thank you, thank you. I love

26   you. *(ADAM grabs her and calms her down.)*

27   **ADAM:** That's not what I meant. Sit down, honey. *(She stops*

28   *screaming and looks at him.)*

29   **JILLIAN:** Why do you want me to sit down?

30   **ADAM:** Just sit please. *(She does.)* OK, now don't get upset, but

31   you didn't get the part. *(Pause)* You're not even called back.

32   *(JILLIAN looks at him, quietly gets up. She goes over to her bag,*

33   *coat and script; throws them one by one at ADAM; and then*

34   *screams and stamps her feet.)* I knew you'd take it well.

35   **JILLIAN:** You want to tell me why?

1   ADAM: Not really, why don't we just leave it at that?

2   JILLIAN: We could do that, but if you don't tell me I'm going to

3   make your life a living hell.

4   ADAM: You wouldn't. *(Pause)* You would. OK, sit down. *(She does.*

5   *He walks tentatively over to her.)* The simple reason is that the

6   director didn't think you were right.

7   JILLIAN: Didn't you tell him I was your girlfriend?

8   ADAM: You told me not to tell him. You didn't even want to meet

9   him. You said you wanted the audition to be just like

10   everybody else's.

11   JILLIAN: I know what I said — I lied. I was just trying to sound

12   noble. Of course you were suppose to tell him! Call him! *Now!*

13   ADAM: I can't do that.

14   JILLIAN: Why not?

15   ADAM: I agree with him. *(JILLIAN starts to look around.)* What are

16   you doing?

17   JILLIAN: Looking for sharp things to throw at you.

18   ADAM: Stop it! Face it — you didn't understand the character.

19   JILLIAN: Are you kidding? I knew her forwards and backwards.

20   ADAM: Really, Mary is a simple, innocent girl-next-door.

21   JILLIAN: I know that.

22   ADAM: Then why did you come out on stage on a Harley, dressed

23   all in leather?

24   JILLIAN: Because that's what Mary wants to do, inside. She wants

25   to be wild.

26   ADAM: Who told you that? I don't even know that and I wrote the

27   damn play.

28   JILLIAN: Nobody told me. I'm a woman and so is Mary. We

29   understand each other.

30   ADAM: Well you and the director don't agree and he's the one

31   who counts. Jilly, this is my first produced play. I have to go

32   with his decisions.

33   JILLIAN: I want to know exactly what he said.

34   ADAM: No, you don't!

35   JILLIAN: *Adam!*

1   ADAM: OK, ... he ... he used the word ... "stinks" a lot. *(Her eyes*
2   *well up and she starts to cry. She sits on the couch and puts her*
3   *head in her hands. ADAM goes and sits next to her.)* **I'm sorry;**
4   **that was cruel.**
5   **JILLIAN: Well, I'm sorry I stink.**
6   **ADAM: Jilly, you don't stink. I told you when you wanted to**
7   **audition that there was really no part for you. If we had**
8   **known each other when I was writing this I could have written**
9   **a part for you.**
10 **JILLIAN: Do you think I stink?**
11 **ADAM: No, I've seen you do some very good work. You have a lot**
12 **of talent. Misdirected as it is sometimes, but still a lot of talent.**
13 **Look, I didn't want to tell you this, but I'm halfway through**
14 **my next play. I wrote the lead for you.**
15 **JILLIAN: Really? Tell me about it.**
16 **ADAM: I'll show you when it's done, but for now I want you to**
17 **know that I love you and I think you're very talented. And I'm**
18 **really sorry this didn't work out better.**
19 **JILLIAN: I love you too.**
20 **ADAM: Feel better?**
21 **JILLIAN: No, but I'll fake it. I am an actress after all.**
22 **ADAM: Fine — want to get some dinner?**
23 **JILLIAN: Sure.** *(ADAM gets up and starts to get his coat.)* **Adam?**
24 **ADAM: What?**
25 **JILLIAN: Have you started casting the part of Larry yet?**
26 **ADAM: Why?**
27 **JILLIAN: Well, if I can't play Mary, maybe I could play Larry.**
28 **ADAM: I give up.** *(He walks out of the room with JILLIAN dogging*
29 *his heels.)*
30 **JILLIAN: No, really, I can play gay ...**
31   **The End**
32
33
34
35

4. Mother

CAST: NANCY, LILY

SCENE OPENS: We are in a living room. Nancy, 30s, is on the couch. She is burned out and obviously quite tired. She has an icepack on her temple. There is a knock at the door.

LILY: *(Off-stage)* **Nancy, are you home?** *(Pause)* **Nancy, it's Mom.**

NANCY: **Mom, who?** *(LILY enters.)*

LILY: **What do you mean, "Mom, who?" How many moms do you have?**

NANCY: **Today, none.**

LILY: **Why?**

NANCY: **Because I realized that no woman would bring a child into this world knowing that someday they might feel like this.**

LILY: **Well. If I must say so, you do look like ...**

NANCY: **Dirt, Mom?**

LILY: **I wasn't going to say that.**

NANCY: **But you were thinking it, right?**

LILY: **Not at all. I was going to say that you looked — tired.**

NANCY: **I am. What are you doing here?**

LILY: **Oh, I see — I have to have a reason to visit my own daughter?**

NANCY: **No, you don't. Sorry. Do you want a cup of coffee?**

LILY: **Thank you, I would.**

NANCY: **Good. When you get yourself a cup, could you get me one too?** *(LILY goes and pours two cups of coffee. She gives one to NANCY.)* **Thanks. So — what can I do for you?**

LILY: **Nothing. I was just in the neighborhood, so I thought I'd stop by.**

NANCY: **In the neighborhood? Mother — you live thirty miles away. How did you just happen to be in the neighborhood?**

LILY: *(Struggling)* **I was shopping at the market.**

NANCY: **Oh, that's right, I forgot that they don't have any food where you live. Come on, Mother — what's up?**

LILY: **Well, to be honest, your father and I have been worried**

1   about you lately.

2   NANCY: Why? There's no reason to.

3   LILY: No reason? Look at yourself, you're exhausted.

4   NANCY: It's Sunday. I'm supposed to be exhausted. If you don't

5   believe me, check your Bible.

6   LILY: What's that supposed to mean?

7   NANCY: Right in Genesis it says: "And God created Sunday and

8   he was exhausted."

9   LILY: Will you be serious?

10   NANCY: Will you? I think I know what this is all about. You and

11   Daddy don't like my lifestyle since I got divorced.

12   LILY: Well. You're right. We don't.

13   NANCY: And what's wrong with it?

14   LILY: For one thing — you're out till all hours. You go out with a

15   lot of different men. In general you're acting like a child. We

16   never see you and we certainly don't know what you're up to.

17   NANCY: And you shouldn't. Mom, I'm over thirty. I don't have to

18   report to you or be in by ten anymore.

19   LILY: Is that any reason to act … act …

20   NANCY: Act what?

21   LILY: … Loose. *(NANCY starts to laugh.)*

22   NANCY: Loose? Can you expand on that?

23   LILY: You know what I'm talking about.

24   NANCY: No, Mother, I don't. Explain.

25   LILY: Where were you last night?

26   NANCY: Here.

27   LILY: Were you alone?

28   NANCY: No.

29   LILY: What were you doing?

30   NANCY: Ah — entertaining.

31   LILY: Entertaining? What does that mean?

32   NANCY: Sex, Mother! I was having sex!

33   LILY: Stop that! Don't use that kind of language. Your father and

34   I never used that word.

35   NANCY: You never did it either.

1   LILY: Fine, make jokes. Next thing you'll be telling me is what bad
2   parents we were.
3   NANCY: I didn't say that, but you were a bit — provincial.
4   LILY: We were not provincial!
5   NANCY: Oh, come on Mother. Because of the way I was brought
6   up, I was a virgin till I was twenty-one.
7   LILY: What's wrong with that?
8   NANCY: I was married at nineteen.
9   LILY: Fine, have it your way. Your father and I ruined your life.
10   NANCY: I didn't say that, but on the other hand, don't condemn
11   my lifestyle because it's not like yours.
12   LILY: I'm not condemning.
13   NANCY: Yes, you are.
14   LILY: It's just that Dad and I are worried since your divorce. You
15   don't seem to have any focus. We just don't want to see you
16   lonely.
17   NANCY: Mother, I'm not. Look, for the first time since I was
18   married I feel good. Work is good. I'm happy.
19   LILY: But what about a husband?
20   NANCY: I *had* a husband. Now I'm experiencing all those things I
21   couldn't by getting married young.
22   LILY: Nancy, you are the most precious thing in the world to Dad
23   and me. We only want what's best for you. A good job, a
24   husband and a family.
25   NANCY: I want those things too. I have the job; the other will
26   come in time, but when I'm ready.
27   LILY: Are you really happy?
28   NANCY: Yes, Mom, I am.
29   LILY: Then I guess that's all that's important. I guess I'll be going.
30   *(She gets up, gives NANCY a hug and kiss and starts to leave.)*
31   NANCY: Mom?
32   LILY: Yes.
33   NANCY: Stop by anytime you're here shopping.
34   **The End**
35

5. The Casting Session

CAST: #1, #2

SCENE OPENS: We are at a casting session. #1, a casting director, is at a desk. There are hundreds of pictures on the table that he/she is looking through. #1 is on a cellular phone.

#1: It's going horribly. *(Pause)* **Because I'm in L.A., that's why.** *(Pause)* **Well, the problem is — there's two million actors in this town, but no talent.** *(Pause)* **Oh, why did I ever leave New York?** *(Pause)* **OK fine, but warm weather doesn't make up for everything.** *(There is a knock on the door and #2 peeks his/her head in.)*

#2: I'm sorry to interrupt, but your assistant said I should come in. *(#1 motions to come in, then speaks into the phone.)*

#1: I'm sorry I've got to cut this short. Another one's just come in. *(Pause)* **Yes, I'll be in for my regular session tomorrow.** *(Pause)* **Thank you, Doctor.** *(#1 hangs up and motions for #2 to come forward.)* **Why don't you come up to the desk? That is unless you care to shout across the room.** *(#2 goes to the desk.)*

#2: Hi, I'm …

#1: Please, no names. Unless you turn out to be a totally wonderful actor, I'd rather you remain anonymous.

#2: *(Pause)* Why?

#1: If I know your name, it becomes personal. I prefer to remain aloof — to remain … distant. I even have my assistant cut the names off all of the pictures.

#2: *(Pause)* I see. *(Pause)* OK … why don't we just read?

#1: Wait! I have to check and see what part you're reading for. *(#1 checks a list.)*

#2: Excuse me, but if you don't know names — how do you check me on a list?

#1: Good question! You know that you're the first one today to question that apparent paradoxical situation. I'm impressed. You're a deep thinker, aren't you?

1   #2: Only if you want me to be.

2   #1: It's what I live for. Anyway, to answer your question, what I do

3   with my list is to have everyone entered by and sent in here at

4   a very specific time. You, for example, are two twenty-six.

5   *(Pause)* I like time. It's free flowing and —

6   #2: Relative?

7   #1: Exactly!! Einstein taught me that.

8   #2: Personally?

9   #1: Yes — but in a past life, of course.

10 #2: Of course. Shall we read? *(#1 is checking the list again.)*

11 #1: Wait! I can't read you.

12 #2: Why not?

13 #1: After checking the list, and meeting you, you're actually not

14   right for the role — or any role in this film for that matter.

15   I'm sorry. You may leave now.

16 #2: *Wait!* What the hell just happened here? You got my picture

17   from my agent, thought I was right, called me in, and *now* you

18   decide I'm wrong for the role?

19 #1: It's simple. Your *picture* emits an aura for a specific part that

20   you don't emit in person. It would be quite the disservice, not

21   to mention a cosmic disaster, if I were to read you.

22 #2: I'll take that chance.

23 #1: I won't.

24 #2: Fine! Whatever! I'm outta here. *(#2 starts to exit. Then, just*

25   *before he/she gets to the door #1 says:)*

26 #1: And if I were you, I'd take some acting classes before I ever

27   auditioned again. You're still a little green. *(#2 stops dead and*

28   *turns slowly back to #1.)*

29 #2: *(Pause)* Excuse me?!

30 #1: I just said that you could use some more seasoning before —

31 #2: I know what you said, but how would you know?! You didn't

32   even hear me read.

33 #1: I don't need to. You put out an amateur's vibe.

34 #2: OK, that tears it. *(#2 looks around, takes a chair and sticks it*

35   *under the doorknob to lock the door and approaches #1.)*

1   #1: What ... what are you doing?
2   #2: What every actor has wanted to do to *some* casting director at
3   *some* point in their career.
4   #1: *(Pause)* Oh, my God! You're going to hit me! *(#2 stops and thinks.)*
5   #2: Actually, I was just going to tell you off, but let's hold on to that
6   hitting thing. It may come in handy. *(#1 backs away from #2.)*
7   #1: If you touch me, I'll sue.
8   #2: Oh, do they have lawyers on your home planet?
9   #1: What?
10 #2: Never mind. Just sit your lame behind down in the chair. I'm
11   not going to touch you, but you are going to get an earful from
12   an indignant actor. *(#1 tentatively slips back into his/her chair.)*
13   Now, where the hell do you get off treating me like this?
14 #1: Well I —
15 #2: Shut up! It was a rhetorical question. I'll have you know that I
16   take my craft very seriously. I researched this part thoroughly,
17   went to my acting coach for two four-hour private sessions,
18   took the day off to properly prepare, and I don't plan to have
19   all that flushed down the toilet because all of a sudden you
20   don't feel my "aura" is correct.
21 #1: May I talk now?
22 #2: Only if you can remain on this astral plane.
23 #1: Fine. In the months that I've been a casting director ...
24 #2: Months?
25 #1: Yes — many months. Anyway, in that time I've found that the
26   actors best suited for a role are the ones that ooze the part
27   from their souls, ooze the part from the hearts, ooze the part
28   from their very pores.
29 #2: OK, see, right here is where we have a problem. Most people I
30   know don't want to ooze anything from their pores. As a
31   matter of fact, most of the people I know — would really
32   prefer to be ooze-free.
33 #1: That's because you probably only know Californians. *(#2 looks*
34   *at #1, then it hits him/her.)*
35 #2: I get it now. You're not from outer space — it's worse — you're

24

1   from New York, right?

2   #1: Of course.

3   #2: I should have known. Only people from there could be this

4   pompous, this arrogant this ... New York.

5   #1: And if you had only spent some time there, it might have made

6   you a better actor. You could have soaked up the overflowing

7   culture that fills New York.

8   #2: The only thing that fills New York is New Yorkers. And I spent

9   three years there. I left the day I was mugged and while reporting

10   it to the police two bums peed on my foot — in the police station.

11   So you'll excuse me if I didn't find any of that cultural.

12   #1: And because you didn't is why you're not ready to audition for

13   me.

14   #2: Oh, I'm ready, and to prove it we're going to read right now.

15   #1: But —

16   #2: No buts. This is not a game show. You have no choice between

17   this or what's behind the curtain. I'm reading.

18   #1: What's the point? I —

19   #2: The point is — remember that hitting thing we talked about?

20   #1: Good point. Read! *(#2 turns and prepares. Suddenly he/she whips*

21   *around and faces #1 and begins the audition.)*

22   #2: "Would you like your check now, or after your coffee?"

23   #1: "After."

24   #2: "Very good." *(#2 turns back to "get out of the moment." #1 rises*

25   *and applauds.)*

26   #1: I'm sorry, I stand corrected. You are marvelous. It must have

27   been that time spent in New York. It did rub off. Well, you

28   have the part! *(#2 looks at #1.)*

29   #2: I've been waiting a long time to do this. Take your part and stick

30   it! *(#2 marches to the door and as his/her hand grabs the knob:)*

31   #1: It pays double scale. *(#2 whips around and heads back to the desk.)*

32   #2: I think you've learned your lesson. Now, about my billing ...

33   *(#2 sits back at the desk.)*

34   **The End**

35

6. The Ghost

CAST: STAN, ALBERT

SCENE OPENS: We are in STAN's apartment. It is late at night. ALBERT is sitting in a chair in the living room. STAN comes into the room with a flashlight. He is looking around.

STAN: Is anybody there? *(Pause)* Is anybody here? *(STAN flashes his light around. It lands on ALBERT. STAN sees him and flicks the lights on.)*

ALBERT: Will you please get that light out of my eyes?

STAN: Who the hell are you?

ALBERT: Considering the situation, that seems like a fair question.

STAN: Are you going to answer it?

ALBERT: In time.

STAN: Fine, I'm calling the police.

ALBERT: There really is no reason to. I'm not armed. I'm not dangerous. *(He stands up, opens his jacket and shows STAN. He stops.)*

STAN: Fine. Then who are you?

ALBERT: Albert.

STAN: Just Albert? No last name? Who do you think you are, Cher?

ALBERT: If it's that important, my last name is Meyers. I'm Albert Meyers.

STAN: Wait a minute. Albert Meyers? My last name is Meyers, and my middle name is Albert.

ALBERT: I know.

STAN: What do you mean "I know"? Who are you?

ALBERT: Answer me this, who were you named for?

STAN: Why?

ALBERT: Just answer.

STAN: OK, I was named for my mother's father, Stanley Plotnick and my father's father, Albert Meyers.

ALBERT: There you have it.

STAN: *Have what?!* All I have is some goof ball in my apartment at

1   two o'clock in the morning who has the same name as my
2   dead grandfather.
3   ALBERT: I don't have the same name as your dead grandfather.
4   *(Pause)* I am your dead grandfather. *(Silence)*
5   STAN: Yeah. OK why don't you just wait here? I'm going to call
6   some people who can help you find your way back to heaven.
7   I'm sure you just took a wrong turn at purgatory and wound
8   up here.
9   ALBERT: I hate this part. Do you know how long it usually takes
10   to convince someone you're a ghost?
11   STAN: Now there's a question I don't get asked everyday. No, I
12   don't and would you please get out of here?! *(ALBERT hands*
13   *him a photo album.)*
14   ALBERT: Look, to save time, just look at this album. *(STAN does.)*
15   Here's a picture of your father and me. Do I look familiar?
16   STAN: OK, there's a resemblance, but that doesn't prove anything.
17   *(ALBERT pulls out a necklace.)*
18   ALBERT: How about this?
19   STAN: My God, that's my father's. He said only he and his ...
20   ALBERT: His what?
21   STAN: His father had one. I have his now. *Oh my God!* You are
22   my grandfather!
23   ALBERT: I'm glad you believe me.
24   STAN: What ... what are you doing here?
25   ALBERT: Do you know how I died?
26   STAN: From what my father told me, you were walking down the
27   street and a piano fell on you.
28   ALBERT: Well, I'm not sure how much you know about heaven,
29   but when you die in a real stupid way —
30   STAN: Like having a piano fall on you?
31   ALBERT: *(Slightly agitated)* Yes, if you must be blunt, like having a
32   piano fall on you, you don't get a lot of respect. You also don't
33   get any of the choice assignments, so I choose to do some extra
34   work to help me gain some respect.
35   STAN: And what's that?

1 ALBERT: To find some hapless human and help him achieve some
2   of his goals.
3 STAN: And *who* might this hapless human be?
4 ALBERT: Whom and — hi there.
5 STAN: I resent that. I am not hapless.
6 ALBERT: Maybe hapless is the wrong term. I mean someone who
7   could use some help.
8 STAN: I don't need any help.
9 ALBERT: Everyone could use a little assistance.
10 STAN: I'm doing fine.
11 ALBERT: Is that all you want to do, just "fine"?
12 STAN: What's wrong with that?
13 ALBERT: Nothing, but you can do better. Everyone in your family
14   has always done "fine," but you can do better. I've watched
15   you for a long time and I know. Don't you want to advance?
16   Don't you want to lead instead of following?
17 STAN: I will. It just takes time.
18 ALBERT: Not if you keep letting others take credit for your work.
19   Stand up for yourself and be counted.
20 STAN: You sound like a commercial.
21 ALBERT: When you've been dead for forty years you miss the
22   latest expressions, but the thought is the same. I'm going to
23   stick around and show you how to assert yourself.
24 STAN: Can anyone else see you?
25 ALBERT: No, that's the beauty of it.
26 STAN: How long did you say you were going to be around?
27 ALBERT: Till you've accomplished your potential. It could be a
28   long or short time. It's up to you.
29 STAN: Why couldn't I have assertiveness training like everyone else?
30 ALBERT: Don't look at it that way; see it as a "godsend."
31 STAN: Great, a funny ghost. I really don't have any say in this, do I?
32 ALBERT: No, so just accept it. We're going to have a good time.
33 STAN: What started out as an ordinary day winds up like
34   something out of *The Twilight Zone*. I'm going to bed. Maybe
35   I'll wake up and find this a dream. Goodnight, Grandpa. *(He*

1   *exits. There is a scream Off-stage.)*
2   **ALBERT:** **I guess I forgot to mention his grandma's here too.**
3   **The End**
4
5
6
7
8
9
10
11
12
13
14
15
16
17
18
19
20
21
22
23
24
25
26
27
28
29
30
31
32
33
34
35

7. The Funeral

CAST: LUCY, SHELLYE

SCENE OPENS: We are at the funeral for Sam Hoff. Seated is LUCY. She was Sam's wife. She is crying or at least making an attempt at it. Enter SHELLYE. She was Sam's niece. She sits, pulls out a tissue, and starts her crying routine. LUCY notices who sitting next to her.

LUCY: **I guess the ghouls come out at funerals.** *(SHELLYE stops crying and notices who she is next to.)*

SHELLYE: **Well, hello Aunt Lucy. I'm surprised to see you here.**

LUCY: **Why? Didn't you think I'd show up at my own husband's funeral?**

SHELLYE: **Yes, but I didn't think the Betty Ford Clinic would let you out until the treatments were finished.**

LUCY: **Witty as usual. Tell me dear, did you come alone or did you bring one of your tricks?**

SHELLYE: **OK, I can see where this is heading, so why don't we cool it? This** *is* **a funeral.**

LUCY: **Yes, it is, and since people with manners, grace, and class usually attend funerals, whatever possessed** *you* **to attend?**

SHELLYE: **If you must know, I came to pay respect to my favorite uncle.**

LUCY: **Favorite, my foot! You never cared about the man while he was alive, why all the concern now?**

SHELLYE: **That's not true. He was warm. He was kind. He was —**

LUCY: *(Interrupting)* **Rich!**

SHELLYE: **This all sounds pretty funny coming from the person who killed him.**

LUCY: **That's a horrible lie.**

SHELLYE: **Really? Wasn't it true that when Uncle Sam came to you complaining of chest pains, you told him it was probably a cold?**

LUCY: **I said that, but when things got worse I called the paramedics.**

1   SHELLYE: Before or after he stopped breathing?
2   LUCY: That's it! *(LUCY stands, throws her purse on the floor, faces*
3   *SHELLYE, and starts yelling.)* OK — listen up! This is a
4   funeral and I would like to bury my husband with some peace
5   and dignity if that is all right with you, you cheap hustler.
6   *(SHELLYE looks around.)*
7   SHELLYE: A little louder, dear, I don't think they heard you in New
8   Jersey. *(LUCY quickly looks around, sits and composes herself.)*
9   LUCY: Why don't you leave? Nobody wants you here.
10 SHELLYE: Actually — Bruce Marshall told me to come.
11 LUCY: Sam's lawyer? Why?
12 SHELLYE: I don't know. He said that he wanted to talk to me
13   after the service.
14 LUCY: Perhaps it has something to do with Sam's will.
15 SHELLYE: *(Getting concerned)* What? Tell me!
16 LUCY: *(Starts to smile.)* I'm sure he wants to warn you that if you
17   are in the will, I plan to contest it.
18 SHELLYE: *(Stands and yells.)* You wouldn't! *(Notices people are*
19   *looking. Sits. Quieter)* You wouldn't.
20 LUCY: Don't bet on it. You forgot that five years ago I gave you a
21   piece of advice.
22 SHELLYE: What was that?
23 LUCY: I reminded you that you *may* be his niece, but I sleep with
24   him. So don't mess with me.
25 SHELLYE: Trust me — I remember.
26 LUCY: You didn't heed my warning, so now you have to pay.
27 SHELLYE: And on what ground do you plan to contest the will?
28 LUCY: I'm not sure, but with your sleazy past, I have a large
29   variety of sleazy items to choose from.
30 SHELLYE: Well, then maybe I'll just have to cause a few problems
31   of my own.
32 LUCY: About what?
33 SHELLYE: About marrying Sam for his money.
34 LUCY: That's ridiculous.
35 SHELLYE: It is? Then explain why you married an eighty-seven-

1   year-old-man, only after finding out that he had a bad heart,

2   bad lungs, and has been impotent for two decades.

3   LUCY: OK — you know why I married the old buzzard and so do

4   I, but just try and bring it out and all it will look like is the

5   jealous niece against the grieving widow. You don't stand a

6   chance. *(She laughs.)*

7   SHELLYE: That stinks!

8   LUCY: Yes, it does, so why don't you slink out the way you came

9   in? *(She stands and starts to walk away.)*

10   SHELLYE: Where are you going — to Rico? *(This stops LUCY in*

11   *her tracks. She goes back to her seat.)*

12   LUCY: *(Nervous)* Who was that?

13   SHELLYE: Rico.

14   LUCY: I don't know whom you're talking about.

15   SHELLYE: You don't? He's been your gardener for five years. You

16   know, tall, good looking, doesn't own any tools — for

17   gardening, that is. Drives a Rolls. You must pay him very well.

18   LUCY: You can't prove a thing.

19   SHELLYE: I'm afraid I can. *(She pulls some photos out of her purse*

20   *and hands them to LUCY.)*

21   SHELLYE: When you gave me your little warning, I decided to

22   keep my eye — and a camera — focused on you. You know,

23   that Little Bo Peep outfit really isn't very flattering on you.

24   Oh — you can keep those. I have plenty.

25   LUCY: What do you want?

26   SHELLYE: Leave my inheritance alone.

27   LUCY: And if I refuse?

28   SHELLYE: Then those photos will have more circulation than the

29   *New York Times.*

30   LUCY: That's extortion!

31   SHELLYE: Lucy, Lucy, extortion's such an ugly word.

32   LUCY: Then what would you call it?

33   SHELLYE: Oh, I call it extortion. But it's such an ugly word.

34   LUCY: Looks like I don't have a choice.

35   SHELLYE: Looks that way.

1   **LUCY: Fine! You'll have no problem with me.**

2   **SHELLYE: I knew you'd see it my way. Always nice to see you,**

3   **dear.** *(SHELLYE gets up and leaves. LUCY watches her go.)*

4   **LUCY:** *Witch!*

5   **The End**

6

7

8

9

10

11

12

13

14

15

16

17

18

19

20

21

22

23

24

25

26

27

28

29

30

31

32

33

34

35

8. The Collector

CAST: #1, #2

SCENE OPENS: We are in #1's apartment. Holiday music is playing. There is a knock at the door. #1 answers it. #2 is there, dressed in Christmas regalia. #1 looks him/her up down.

#1: Uh ... hi there.

#2: Hi. Happy holidays.

#1: And happy holidays to you too. Can I help you?

#2: You certainly can. I'm Murray/Mary the elf, and —

#1: Excuse me, did you say Murray/Mary the elf?

#2: Yes, I did.

#1: That's what I thought. OK ... Murray/Mary, go on.

#2: Santa has sent me to ask you if you would care to donate to the Homeless Children's Fund.

#1: What's the Homeless Children's Fund?

#2: The Homeless Children's Fund collects money to buy toys for the homeless children of our city who would otherwise get nothing come Christmas or Hanukkah or Kwanzaa.

#1: Well, that sounds wonderful. Come on in. *(#2 enters.)* Why don't you wait here and I'll get you a check. *(Pause)* Oh, Santa does accept checks, doesn't he?

#2: Of course he does. Santa trusts all the children in the world. The young and the ... not so young.

#1: Does he now? Well, that's ... great. Wait here. I'll be right back. *(#1 goes to the desk and writes a check. #2 looks around.)*

#2: This is a nice place you have. Santa would like it very much.

#1: I'm so pleased. Here you go. *(#1 hands #2 a check. #2 reaches into the bag he/she is carrying and pulls out a candy cane and hands it to #1.)*

#2: And here you go. Santa thanks you for your generosity.

#1: Yeah, whatever. Glad I could help. I'll walk you out. *(#1 starts to walk #2 out. #2 takes a look at the check and stops.)*

#2: Whoa, wait a minute.

1   #1: What? Something wrong?

2   #2: Yes, I think you made a mistake. This check is for ten dollars.

3   #1: I know. I'm giving you ten dollars.

4   #2: I see. Gosh, you know, I don't think Santa's going to be very

5   happy with this.

6   #1: Ask me if I care. Look, does the phrase "looking a gift horse in

7   the mouth" mean anything to you?

8   #2: Yes. Does the phrase "cheap as all get out" mean anything to you?

9   #1: *Excuse me?!*

10 #2: Let me ask you something. Do you know what you can buy for

11   ten dollars?

12 #1: I don't know ... stuff?

13 #2: Stuff? *Stuff?!* Well, let me welcome you to the twenty-first

14   century, friend. For ten bucks you get nada. Get it? Nothing!

15   A bow for Barbie's hair costs at least twenty.

16 #1: Look, that's not my problem. Why don't you just take the

17   check I gave you and get out of here? *(#2 closes the door.)*

18 #2: I don't think so. I'm going to give you one more chance to do

19   the right thing and write me another check.

20 #1: And I'm going to give you one chance to get your butt back to

21   the North Pole before I call the cops. *(#1 moves towards the*

22   *phone.)*

23 #2: I wouldn't do that if I were you. *(#2 reaches into the bag he/she*

24   *is holding.)*

25 #1: What are you going to do, candy cane me to death?

26 #2: Not exactly. *(#2 pulls out a gun. #1 jumps back.)*

27 #1: *Are you nuts?!* What the hell do you think you're doing!!??

28 #2: I don't think, I know. And what I know is that I've just become

29   your worst nightmare. I'm an elf with a pistol, so don't mess

30   with me! Sit your cheap butt down. *(#1 sits down in a chair.)*

31 #1: I don't believe this. I'm being mugged by an elf.

32 #2: No. Let's get this straight. You are not being mugged.

33 #1: Really? And what would you call being held at gunpoint, in my

34   own apartment.

35 #2: I call it making you see the error of your ways.

1 #1: What did I do that was so wrong? What was my "error"? I gave
2   you money for the kids. That's a good thing, isn't it?
3 #2: If you lived in a cardboard box outside the bus station, ten
4   dollars would be great. But look around this place. Look at
5   your neighborhood.
6 #1: OK, but it's not a crime to live in a nice place.
7 #2: It is if you don't share the wealth just a bit more. How can you
8   look at yourself in the mirror knowing you have so much and
9   they have so little? How can you sleep at night knowing that
10   the only toy little Tommy or little Suzy probably has is a dead
11   rat they found in the garbage? And you think ten dollars can
12   fix that?
13 #1: Aren't you exaggerating just a bit?
14 #2: Excuse me? Are you calling me a liar? I'm standing here with a
15   gun explaining how you rich people get through life by
16   walking over the less fortunate, and you're calling me a liar?
17   Does that seem like a wise thing to do?
18 #1: Probably not. OK, here's what we will do. You get me my
19   checkbook from the desk and I'll write you a new check.
20   How's that?
21 #2: It depends. *(#2 gets the checkbook and gives it to #1.)* If you put
22   at least three zeros it'll be perfect.
23 #1: *A thousand dollars!?* *(#2 waves the gun around.)*
24 #2: As I see it, you really don't have much of a choice — do you?
25 #1: *(Pause)* A thousand it is. *(#1 starts to write the check.)* Whatever
26   happened to just being naughty or nice?
27 #2: You think anybody really cares about that anymore?
28 #1: I did when I was a kid.
29 #2: Really. Then how come you used to tease that little girl/boy,
30   Sally/Billy, all the time? Or steal things from the five and
31   dime?
32 #1: Wait a minute, how did you know …
33 #2: Or how about cheating on your taxes for the last three years, or
34   that bank account the IRS doesn't know about. Those would
35   make you very naughty, but you don't care, do you?

1   #1: *(Pause)* **How do you know all that?**
2   #2: **You think I'd dress like this if I didn't have to?**
3   #1: **Are you trying to tell me that you're a real ... real ...**
4   #2: **Elf. The word's elf. And yes, I am. Trust me, I wanted to be a**
5   **lawyer, but my father made me go into the family business.**
6   **Now, give me the damn check!** *(#1 hands #2 the check. #2 looks*
7   *it over.)* **There, that's much better. Doesn't giving a lot make**
8   **you feel good?**
9   #1: **Well ...**
10 #2: **Just say "yes" so I can get out of here.**
11 #1: **Yes.**
12 #2: **I knew it would. Now, you have a good holiday and remember ...**
13   **we're always watching. Bye now.** *(#2 exits. #1 looks around the*
14   *room.)*
15 #1: *(Pause)* **I need a drink.** *(#1 starts to make a drink.)*
16   **The End**
17
18
19
20
21
22
23
24
25
26
27
28
29
30
31
32
33
34
35

9. The Lawsuit

CAST: #1, #2

SCENE OPENS: We are in an apartment. There is a knock at the door. #1 comes out of the bedroom and goes to and answers the door. #2 is there.

#2: Hi there. Mr./Ms. Chambers, right?

#1: Yes.

#2: Mind if I come in? *(#2 just sort of pushes his/her way into the apartment and looks around.)* **Hey, nice place. It's amazing what they can do with low-cost housing nowadays, isn't it?**

#1: Excuse me! Who are you?! *(Pause)* ***What are you?!*** *(#2 takes out a card and hands it to #1.)*

#2: Marshall. Jamie Marshall.

#1: That name sounds familiar. Do I know you?

#2: No, not personally. *(#1 thinks for a moment.)*

#1: Wait a minute! Aren't you that ambulance-chasing lawyer who's always advertising on TV? The one who dresses up in a cowboy outfit and says ...

#2: ... and says, "Hi, there. I'm Jamie Marshall, the marshal of law. I make the bad guys pay."

#1: Yeah, that's the one. You're pretty ... unbelievable.

#2: Thank you.

#1: Don't thank me. I'm not sure it was a compliment. I do have to ask you something. Did you really get that one guy seven million?

#2: Which guy?

#1: The one on your commercial who got run over by a zebra during a circus parade.

#2: Oh, him. Sure did.

#1: You got him seven million dollars?

#2: No. I didn't say dollars.

#1: Then what did you get him?

#2: Pennies.

1   #1: *Pennies?!* You got him seven million pennies? That's what ...
2   seventy thousand dollars? It's hardly the same thing.
3   #2: But it's not bad considering the guy was stupid enough to get
4   run over by a zebra. True?
5   #1: So, what do you want with me? *(#2 pulls out a note pad and*
6   *starts checking it.)*
7   #2: Were you over at the Pantry Market about a half hour ago?
8   #1: *(Tentative)* Yeah.
9   #2: So was I. You took a fall in aisle seven. Right in front of the
10   creamed corn, right? *(#2 looks up. #1 is sort of staring*
11   *incredulously.)*
12   #1: Oh my God! You don't chase ambulances. You chase shopping
13   carts.
14   #2: Now wait a minute. I saw the whole thing. You got a great case.
15   #1: Forget it. See that over there? That's called a door. I'd love it if
16   you were on the other side of it. Now! *(#1 starts to walk away.*
17   *#2 jumps in front of him/her.)*
18   #2: Look, I know what you think of me, but the facts are you fell in
19   that store and they should pay.
20   #1: The floor was a little slippery, and I stumbled. The manager
21   came over, asked me if I were OK and told them not to charge
22   me for my milk.
23   #2: Milk? *MILK?!* And that makes it OK. I saw you fall. Do you
24   know how close you were to losing your life? You were staring
25   death in the eye and it was saying, "Come to me Terry/Terri
26   Chambers for your time has come and you are mine" and you
27   think that can be bought off with a carton of milk?
28   #1: A little melodramatic, aren't we?
29   #2: Not at all. And it doesn't just stop at you.
30   #1: It doesn't?
31   #2: No. What if it weren't you who slipped? What if next time it's a
32   child ... or ... a   mother ... or ... worse   yet,   someone's
33   grandmother who slips on that spot?
34   #1: Grandmother?
35   #2: Just follow me here. Yes, someone's ... eighty-year-old grandmother.

| 1 | #1: | Eighty. Old enough to be old, but not ancient. |

1 #1: Eighty. Old enough to be old, but not ancient.
2 #2: You're catching on. Eighty-year-old granny who probably had to
3   escape the war in Europe in the thirties. Granny who came to
4   America, made it through the depression and world wars,
5   Granny who finally settled down and raised a big family,
6   believing in the American dream. Suppose it is she who slips?
7 #1: I am truly fascinated. Go on.
8 #2: Well, being eighty she probably wouldn't survive a fall like you
9   had. Then where would all those children, grandchildren, and
10   great-grandchildren go on Thanksgiving and Christmas? An
11   entire family would be ripped asunder. A woman who
12   survived the horrors of war would meet her untimely demise
13   in front of the cheese doodles ...
14 #1: Creamed corn.
15 #2: Whatever, and it would be your fault because you wouldn't
16   help teach these people a lesson.
17 #1: That is the biggest bunch of crap I've ever heard.
18 #2: I'll have you know that speech got Dory Schneider half a
19   million when I used it as a closing argument. And that time it
20   *wasn't* pennies.
21 #1: And what exactly did you get for that philanthropic endeavor?
22 #2: Thirty-three percent. What I always get. And it's on contingency.
23 #1: Get out of here. *(#2 pulls out a piece of paper.)*
24 #2: You know Mr./Ms. Chamber, according to your TRW you're
25   not exactly in the financial position to turn me down.
26 #1: Let me see that. *(#1 grabs the paper from #2.)* Wait, this is my
27   credit report! How did you get this?
28 #2: After I got your name, I plugged my laptop modem into my
29   cellular phone, tapped the DMV records, got your social security
30   number then called up TRW and got this report. I printed it out
31   on my portable printer. Isn't technology wonderful?
32 #1: This is illegal. I could sue, you know.
33 #2: Great, I'll represent you. *(Pause)* Still, the facts are, you have a
34   lot of debts and you can hardly afford to turn down two
35   hundred and fifty thousand dollars.

1 #1: I don't care ... *(Pause)* How much did you say?
2 #2: Two hundred and fifty thousand dollars.
3 #1: How do you figure?
4 #2: We sue for a million. They'll offer one hundred thousand
5   dollars. We'll say two-fifty and they'll settle.
6 #1: How do you know?
7 #2: Pantry Market's a big company, nation-wide. This would be a
8   nuisance suit. Two-fifty is nothing for them.
9 #1: And you're sure about this?
10 #2: Look, I have four homes across the country. I drive a Mercedes
11   and a Ferrari and you ... don't. Need I say any more? *(#1*
12   *starts to think.)*
13 #1: You know ... where I fell today ...
14 #2: Yes ...
15 #1: It is starting to get somewhat sore.
16 #2: Where?
17 #1: My hip joint.
18 #2: Hip joint, that's very good. Is it affecting the way ... no, let me
19   rephrase that. It *is* affecting the way you walk, right?
20 #1: Absolutely! See? *(#1 starts doing an injured walk.)*
21 #2: That's very good. I'll tell you, that hip looks degenerative. You
22   may need a walker by the time we get to court.
23 #1: A walker?! Really!? That's great! *(#1 continues the injured walk,*
24   *getting even more dramatic.)* I'm not sure, but I think it's
25   starting to affect my spine. Also, did I tell you about *my*
26   grandmother?
27 #2: Tell me.
28 #1: She's ninety-seven and on dialysis that I pay for. If I can't
29   work, neither will her kidneys.
30 #2: Dialysis, you're very good. *(#1 continues as we fade out.)*
31   **The End**
32
33
34
35

10. The Drawing Room

CAST: SAMANTHA, BROOKE

SCENE OPENS: SAMANTHA is seated at a table in her apartment. She checks her watch once, then again. Finally she gets up and begins to get ready to go out. She gets her jacket and bag, and as she's about to exit, BROOKE enters. BROOKE definitely has a New York upbringing and the accent to prove it.

SAMANTHA: Well, it's about time. Another thirty seconds and I would have been gone.

BROOKE: I'm sorry, but as you're always telling me, I'm always a minute short and a day late.

SAMANTHA: That's fine for you, but now you're affecting my whole day. Well, never mind, you're here now. What's so important that I had to give up my aerobics class?

BROOKE: I need a big favor from you.

SAMANTHA: So I gathered from your phone call.

BROOKE: Yeah, I have an audition and I need your help to learn how to speak proper.

SAMANTHA: Speak properly!

BROOKE: See, you're the perfect teacher. You can be my Henry Higgins.

SAMANTHA: I'm not sure I appreciate the comparison, but I'll give it a try. *(They both sit.)*

BROOKE: Great!

SAMANTHA: First, what's the play, and second, when's the audition?

BROOKE: The audition is tomorrow and the play is *The Drawing Room*.

SAMANTHA: *The Drawing Room*?! Roger Wainright's new play? How did you get an audition for that? I've been trying to get in on that for a month.

BROOKE: My agents showed the director my picture and he told her that he wanted to see me.

1 SAMANTHA: I take it he hasn't heard you speak yet?

2 BROOKE: No, he hasn't. That's why I need your help. I figure if

3   anyone could teach me that Noel Coward, Roger Wainright

4   type of stuff, you can.

5 SAMANTHA: What?

6 BROOKE: You know what I mean. All those people in those plays

7   are so uptight. They all walk and talk like they've got poles up

8   their butts.

9 SAMANTHA: Brooke — has anyone ever told you that you have a

10   charming vocabulary?

11 BROOKE: Yeah, my boyfriend.

12 SAMANTHA: Bruno?

13 BROOKE: Yeah.

14 SAMANTHA: It figures.

15 BROOKE: So, are you going to help me, Sammy?

16 SAMANTHA: Not if you call me Sammy.

17 BROOKE: OK, will you help me — Samantha?

18 SAMANTHA: Well, I must admit it *will* be a challenge.

19 BROOKE: Here's the scene I'm reading tomorrow. *(She gives*

20   *SAMANTHA the script and SAMANTHA looks it over.)*

21 SAMANTHA: *(In a proper British accent)* This is really quite simple.

22 BROOKE: That's great!

23 SAMANTHA: I know. You see, you must remember that these are

24   proper people. It's as if every word they speak is carefully

25   chosen and pronounced.

26 BROOKE: OK, I understand. *(SAMANTHA shows BROOKE the*

27   *script.)*

28 SAMANTHA: Now — you are Pamela. Remember what I just told

29   you. Now — how would you say this line?

30 BROOKE: I wouldn't say that line.

31 SAMANTHA: What?

32 BROOKE: I wouldn't say that line. Look at this. *(Reading)* "I'm so

33   pleased to make your acquaintance. I hope you're finding

34   your stay a pleasant one." Who talks like that?

35 SAMANTHA: Roger Wainright's people do. What would you say?

1   BROOKE: I don't know. *(Pause)* How about, "Nice to see ya.
2   How's it going?"
3   SAMANTHA: *(Dropping the accent)* "Nice to see ya, how's it
4   going?" You've got to be kidding.
5   BROOKE: Why?
6   SAMANTHA: Because you're auditioning for Pamela and this is
7   how she speaks.
8   BROOKE: *(Getting angry)* Well, it's a dumb way to talk. I am not
9   going to do it.
10   SAMANTHA: I should have my head examined trying to teach
11   proper English to a person with the grammatical patterns of
12   Rocky!
13   BROOKE: Is that how you feel about it?
14   SAMANTHA: Yes.
15   BROOKE: Then why don't we just forget the whole thing?
16   SAMANTHA: That suits me fine.
17   BROOKE: Me too, bye! *(BROOKE picks up her things and starts to*
18   *exit.)*
19   SAMANTHA: *Halt!* *(BROOKE stops at the door.)* First off, you
20   forgot your script. Second, I won that argument too easily.
21   BROOKE: What are you talking about?
22   SAMANTHA: I've known you for a long time, Brooke. You don't
23   want to do well tomorrow.
24   BROOKE: You're crazy.
25   SAMANTHA: Am I? Come on, Brooke. Be straight with me.
26   What's wrong?
27   BROOKE: I *am* and nothing's wrong!
28   SAMANTHA: There is too.
29   BROOKE: There is not!
30   SAMANTHA: *Yes there is* — now tell me! *(Silence)*
31   BROOKE: *(Softly)* Fine — I'll tell you. *(Pause)* I'm terrified.
32   SAMANTHA: Terrified of what?
33   BROOKE: I've been acting since I was five years old, but all the
34   parts I've gotten I could have slept through. Now I've got a
35   chance to stretch myself as an actress and I'm scared I won't

1	succeed, that I'll be — laughed at. If that happens — I don't
2	know if I could take it.
3	SAMANTHA: I don't mean to minimize your fears, but you're
4	hardly alone. You very well may be laughed at. Then again —
5	you may be brilliant. You're too good an actress not to try. I
6	think you can do it, but that's not really important if you
7	don't think so.
8	BROOKE: So, you think I should go for it?
9	SAMANTHA: Absolutely. At least it'll stop you from doing plays
10	like, *Biker Heaven* for a while. *(They both laugh, then hug.)*
11	BROOKE: I knew you'd be my Henry Higgins. *(SAMANTHA takes*
12	*the script, opens it and motions for BROOKE to take a seat.)*
13	SAMANTHA: "I'm so please to make your acquaintance. I hope
14	you're finding your stay a pleasant one." Repeat. Please.
15	*(BROOKE starts to repeat as the lights fade.)*
16	**The End**
17	
18	
19	
20	
21	
22	
23	
24	
25	
26	
27	
28	
29	
30	
31	
32	
33	
34	
35	

11. The Conference

CAST: #1, #2

SCENE OPENS: We are in an elementary school. #1 is a school counselor. He/she is seated at a desk. #2, a parent, enters.

#2: Mr./Miss Atkins. I'm sorry if I'm late.

#1: Not at all, Mr./Mrs. Parker. Please come in and sit down. *(#2 sits.)* I was hoping to talk to you and your husband/wife about Bobby.

#2: He/she is out of town on business. I'm sure I can handle whatever the little problem is.

#1: Unfortunately, I wouldn't call it a "little" problem.

#2: Oh. Is Bobby still having problems with that Johnson boy?

#1: No. As a matter of fact, they've become friends.

#2: Then what's the problem?

#1: *(Pause)* Is everything all right at home?

#2: Yes. Why do you ask?

#1: Sometimes when there are problems at home, a child may start to act … oddly.

#2: Bobby hasn't been acting oddly.

#1: Maybe not at home.

#2: He's been acting oddly at school?

#1: Yes. He's starting to frighten his teacher a little.

#2: He's seven years old. What could he possible be doing that would frighten his teacher?

#1: He's a devil worshipper. *(Silence. Then #2 starts to chuckle.)*

#2: I'm sorry. I must not have heard you correctly. It sounded like you said my son was a —

#1: Devil worshipper. I did.

#2: You know, if this is some kind of joke, it's in very poor taste.

#1: I wish it were a joke, but it's not.

#2: My son is seven years old!

#1: I know how old Bobby is, but it doesn't change my opinion.

#2: And what makes you qualified to make these conclusions? You're a grade school guidance counselor.

1   **#1:** And I am also a qualified and licensed child psychologist. But
2   even if I wasn't, the signs are plain enough to see.
3   **#2:** What signs?
4   **#1:** Last week during a sing-along in music class, Bobby got up and
5   asked everyone to join him in "Row, row, row your boat."
6   **#2:** So?
7   **#1:** So, he changed the lyrics slightly. *(#1 pulls out a sheet of paper*
8   *and reads.)* "Row, row, row your boat, down the River Styx. It
9   leads up to Satan's door. The number's six-six-six."
10   **#2:** Oh, come on! He probably heard it on MTV or ... or Sesame
11   Street or something.
12   **#1:** *Sesame Street?!*
13   **#2:** Yeah, you know, they were probably doing a show on the number
14   six and sang that song or something. But it doesn't mean —
15   **#1:** Then how about his report?
16   **#2:** Oh, no. What report?
17   **#1:** Bobby's class was asked to write a report on what they did
18   during vacation. Don't you check his homework?
19   **#2:** No ... uh ... not always. *(#1 hands #2 the paper.)*
20   **#1:** Why don't you read it now? *(#2 takes it and starts to read.)*
21   **#2:** "My trip. By Bobby Parker. We went to visit Grandma and
22   Grandpa on Easter." So? I don't see ...
23   **#1:** Keep reading.
24   **#2:** "Mommy and Daddy and Jenny, that's my sister, and me got in
25   the car and drove to Grandma's and Grandpa's. We saw a lot
26   of things. On the way I asked Daddy if we could stop and visit
27   ... uh ... visit ... "
28   **#1:** Visit what, Mr./Mrs. Parker? Please read.
29   **#2:** " ... If we could stop and visit Hell! Mr. Satan is the boss of Hell
30   and ... "
31   **#1:** Enough said? This is a public school Mr./Mrs. Parker. I think
32   you can imagine how this has upset the teachers.
33   **#2:** Yeah, I've got a picture, but I don't understand any of this.
34   **#1:** Did Bobby ask you what a "pure child" was?
35   **#2:** Uh, no, he didn't.

1   #1: Well, a few days ago he came to school and asked some of his
2   friends if they were "pure children." When his teacher asked
3   what he was doing, he told her that he needed to sacrifice a
4   pure child at the "Dark of the Moon Ceremony" and he was
5   just trying to find one. That poor woman collapsed.
6   #2: This is all very confusing.
7   #1: And you haven't noticed anything … unusual at home?
8   #2: Well, lately he has been talking to an imaginary friend. But he's
9   had them before.
10 #1: Really?
11 #2: Yes. When he was five he used to talk with Mr. Bunny all the
12   time.
13 #1: Well it appears that Mr. Bunny has been replaced by Mr.
14   Beelzebub and I think it warrants a bit more attention.
15 #2: So, what do you think he needs? A lecture, counseling … an
16   exorcism?
17 #1: No, nothing that drastic, but I don't think counseling would
18   hurt. We just want to find out where he's getting these ideas.
19 #2: Do you have any suggestions on who we should take him to?
20 #1: Yes, I have a list. Let me get it for you. *(#1 goes to a filing cabinet*
21   *and pulls out a list.)* I think the "Gate Master" will get along
22   with any of these people.
23 #2: The who?
24 #1: The "Gate Master." It's the name Bobby insists on being called
25   now.
26 #2: Why does that sound so familiar? *(#2 thinks, then remembers.)*
27   "The Gate Master!" It's a video game.
28 #1: I don't understand.
29 #2: Bobby had his birthday a little while ago. We had a party and one
30   of his friends gave him a video game called "The Gate Master."
31   Bobby said it's a kind of Dungeons and Dragons game.
32 #1: Where does the game take place?
33 #2: I don't know. I know I should have looked at it, but I'm willing
34   to bet it takes place … well, not here.
35 #1: Does he get into video games?

1   #2: Are you kidding? We got him a race car game and for two
2   months he told everyone his name was Jeff Gordon. I think I
3   can handle this.
4   #1: I'm not sure ...
5   #2: Well, I am. Let me try, and if it doesn't work, we'll try your
6   way. Fair?
7   #1: Very fair.
8   #2: Thanks for your concern.
9   #1: That's my job. *(#2 starts to exit, then turns back.)*
10 #2: Of course, if we're wrong, and he really is the "Gate Keeper,"
11   you all may want to be very nice to him. *(#2 smiles at #1 and*
12   *exits. #1 pulls a garlic necklace or some other protective "object"*
13   *from a drawer.)*
14   **The End**
15
16
17
18
19
20
21
22
23
24
25
26
27
28
29
30
31
32
33
34
35

12. The Morning After

CAST: JIMMY, TOBI

SCENE OPENS: We are in a hotel suite. TOBI is sitting on the couch reading the paper and having a cup of coffee. JIMMY enters from the bedroom. He enters groaning and generally not doing very well.

TOBI: Good morning. *(She looks up and sees him.)* God, Jimmy, you look awful.

JIMMY: You should see it from my side.

TOBI: You want some coffee? *(He sits next to her.)*

JIMMY: Oh, yeah! Intravenously if possible.

TOBI: You poor thing. Wait here. *(She gets up and pours him some coffee.)*

JIMMY: I couldn't go anywhere if I wanted to. *(TOBI brings the coffee back to him and sits down.)*

TOBI: When are you going to learn that you can't drink?

JIMMY: I think last night might have driven the point home. *(Pause)* Still, Jack and ...

TOBI: Denise.

JIMMY: Denise had a great wedding, didn't they?

TOBI: It was beautiful. Tell me, how much do you remember?

JIMMY: Oh, I wasn't that bad.

TOBI: Wanna bet?

JIMMY: I remember the ceremony, most of the reception, giving the best man speech ...

TOBI: How about after Jack and Denise left?

JIMMY: I'm a little fuzzy. What happened?

TOBI: I told you I thought we should come back to the hotel and I should put you to bed.

JIMMY: Aw, you're always taking care of me, aren't you? *(He takes her hand and gives her a kiss.)*

TOBI: Yes, I am, but you didn't want to come straight back.

JIMMY: We went somewhere else?

TOBI: Yeah, and I didn't think you'd remember.

1   JIMMY: So, where'd we go?

2   TOBI: Well ... we ... *(JIMMY notices something on TOBI's hand.)*

3   JIMMY: Hey, what's this? Is it new?

4   TOBI: Yes, it's a new ring. I got it last night.

5   JIMMY: Funny, it kinda looks like ... like a ...

6   TOBI: Like a what?

7   JIMMY: Like a wedding ring?

8   TOBI: It does, doesn't it? Well, I'm going to get some more coffee.

9   *(She gets up, goes to the coffee pot and pours herself some more*

10   *coffee.)*

11   JIMMY: Why are you wearing what looks like a wedding ring.

12   You're not going to tell me we got married?

13   TOBI: No, not if you don't want me to.

14   JIMMY: Good!

15   TOBI: But we did. *(JIMMY almost chokes on the coffee he's drinking.*

16   *TOBI goes back and sits next to him.)*

17   JIMMY: What?! We got married? I don't understand.

18   TOBI: It's a very simple concept. We're married. Two syllables, an

19   adjective meaning "of marriage, being husband and wife."

20   That's according to Mr. Webster, anyway.

21   JIMMY: Why ... how ... I ... you ...

22   TOBI: I'll try and explain. On the way back in the cab, you took

23   my face in your hands, looked at me, kissed me and said:

24   "Tobi, I love you more than anyone in the world. I want to

25   spend my life with you. As long as we're in Vegas ... let's do it.

26   Let's get married."

27   JIMMY: And you took that as a proposal?

28   TOBI: What can I say, but "Oh, dopey me."

29   JIMMY: Did I say anything else.

30   TOBI: You started to, but decided to throw up instead.

31   JIMMY: I don't believe it. I was drunk and you took advantage of

32   me.

33   TOBI: How could I take advantage when it was your idea? I just

34   went along with it.

35   JIMMY: So we just went to one of those quickie chapels and got

1   married?

2   **TOBI:** Not exactly. See, at the first one ...

3   **JIMMY:** First one!? How many did we go to?

4   **TOBI:** Five.

5   **JIMMY:** *Five?!* What the hell for? *(TOBI picks up an envelope on*

6   *the table and takes out the documents inside. She hands one to*

7   *JIMMY.)* **What's this?**

8   **TOBI:** Our marriage license. *(JIMMY reads it over.)*

9   **JIMMY:** This says you married Errol Flynn.

10   **TOBI:** See what I had to put up with? Now, from there I married ...

11   *(She hands him another license.)*

12   **JIMMY:** Orson Wells ... *(She hands him another)* **Esther Williams?!**

13   Couldn't you have married anyone from the later half of the

14   twentieth century? *(She holds up a finger telling him to wait and*

15   *hands him another. He reads it over.)* **John F. Kennedy.**

16   **TOBI:** That was my favorite. I always wanted to be First Lady.

17   **JIMMY:** So what you're telling me is that these are all jokes ...

18   *(She hands him a last license. He looks it over)* **or not.** *(Pause)*

19   God, we're married.

20   **TOBI:** You needn't say it like you were just informed of a tax audit.

21   **JIMMY:** Did I at least get a honeymoon night?

22   **TOBI:** In your condition? Yeah, get real.

23   **JIMMY:** So we never really consummated the whole thing, did we?

24   **TOBI:** What are you doing, looking for a loophole?

25   **JIMMY:** I don't believe it.

26   **TOBI:** Look, honey, I started to go along as just a gag, but then I

27   thought, "Why not?" We were getting married next year

28   anyway, unless you were planning on backing out.

29   **JIMMY:** No, I wasn't, but ...

30   **TOBI:** But, what?

31   **JIMMY:** I was hoping it would be different, more ... memorable.

32   **TOBI:** Trust me, I'll never forget it. What else would you have

33   wanted?

34   **JIMMY:** To be conscious during the ceremony would have been a

35   plus ... maybe have our friends there.

1   TOBI: So we'll have a big party when we get home. Tell me
2   something. Do you love me?
3   JIMMY: Yes.
4   TOBI: And I love you. So what's the big deal, 'cause whether we're
5   married or not, the end result's the same.
6   JIMMY: And that is?
7   TOBI: I'm stuck with you and you're blessed with me. What could
8   be more perfect? *(He kisses her.)*
9   JIMMY: True.
10 TOBI: So, how you feeling?
11 JIMMY: OK. Why?
12 TOBI: You've got a wedding night to make up for.
13 JIMMY: I do, don't I?
14 TOBI: So how about it, John?
15 JIMMY: That's Mr. President to you. *(Pause)* Can I bring Errol
16   and Orson with us?
17 TOBI: Why not? The more the merrier. *(They get up and start*
18   *towards the bedroom.)*
19 JIMMY: Did I really throw up on you?
20 TOBI: Actually, it was more like the back of the cab, Las Vegas
21   Boulevard ...
22   **The End**
23
24
25
26
27
28
29
30
31
32
33
34
35

13. The Plan

CAST: KAREN, BOBBY

SCENE OPENS: BOBBY is in his apartment. He is sitting on the couch doing some work. There is an excited knock on the door.

KAREN: *(Off-stage)* **Bobby! Bobby, are you there? It's me. Open up.** *(Bobby gets up and answers the door.)*

BOBBY: **Where the have you been, Karen? I've been trying to find you for three days. I've left you forty-eight messages.**

KAREN: **That's not entirely true, you only left one message.**

BOBBY: **What?**

KAREN: **OK, granted, you left it forty-eight times, but it was only one message.**

BOBBY: **Don't mess with me. Where have you been?**

KAREN: **There's something I needed to figure out and I needed some time alone.**

BOBBY: **Well, I wish you'd have told me. I was worried about you.**

KAREN: **You're always looking out for me, aren't you?**

BOBBY: **Hey, everyone needs a hobby. Besides, what are best friends for?** *(Pause)* **So, did you figure out whatever it was?**

KAREN: **Yes, and I need to talk to you about it.**

BOBBY: **OK. Why don't we go to dinner and talk? Maybe catch a movie.**

KAREN: *(Pause)* **Bobby, I want to have a baby.**

BOBBY: *(Pause)* **Oh, a movie would be so much cheaper.**

KAREN: **I'm serious, Bobby. I'm going to have a baby.**

BOBBY: **What do you mean, "I'm going to have a baby"? Did you get pregnant since Friday?**

KAREN: **No, but I'm planning to get that way.**

BOBBY: **Really? Do you have anyone picked out or are you going to go downtown and say to the first guy you like, "Hi, I'm Karen Miller. Will you impregnate me?"**

KAREN: **Will you stop?**

BOBBY: **Will you? You're talking crazy.**

1 KAREN: I'm not talking crazy. This is what I really want.
2 BOBBY: Fine. I know that you've wanted a baby for a while, but
3   need I remind you that you're not married? Hell, you're not
4   even seeing anyone at the moment.
5 KAREN: Trust me, I know that and a guy isn't really necessary.
6 BOBBY: He isn't? Great. When you have this child make sure you
7   let the church know. They can proclaim it a new holiday and
8   call it "Christmas II: A New Beginning."
9 KAREN: You know what I mean.
10 BOBBY: Yes, and it's frightening. *(Pause)*You're not really
11   thinking of artificial insemination, are you?
12 KAREN: The process I want is called "in vitro fertilization" and it
13   means that I —
14 BOBBY: I *know* what it is, but come on, Karen, you don't want to
15   do it this way.
16 KAREN: Yes, I do! I told you I've been thinking about this for a
17   while. This is not a rash decision.
18 BOBBY: Uh-huh.
19 KAREN: Don't "uh-huh" me. I've come to the realization that I'm
20   not good in relationships. They don't last that long, and I
21   can't stand most of the guys I've been involved with, but I still
22   want kids.
23 BOBBY: So — what are you planning? *(KAREN looks directly into*
24   *BOBBY's eyes.)*
25 KAREN: Bob, I want your help. *(BOBBY doesn't move. He stares*
26   *blankly back at KAREN.)*
27 BOBBY: *(Pause)* I need a drink. *(He starts to go, but KAREN pulls*
28   *him back.)*
29 KAREN: You don't need a drink.
30 BOBBY: Karen, you come in here after being missing for three
31   days, tell me that you're going to have a baby, proceed to
32   explain you're going to use in vitro fertilization, and to top it
33   *all* off you say you want my help. If *that* doesn't *require* a
34   drink, nothing ever will. *(He starts to head out.)*
35 KAREN: Well, are you going to do it?

1   **BOBBY:** What? ... *No!*

2   **KAREN:** Why not?! *(BOBBY walks back to her.)*

3   **BOBBY:** Why not? Outside of being the craziest thing you've ever

4   suggested, you ... never return anything you borrow!

5   **KAREN:** What?!

6   **BOBBY:** Go ahead, deny it. Remember that Springsteen album

7   you borrowed two years ago.

8   **KAREN:** You wanna give me a real reason why not?

9   **BOBBY:** I don't have to.

10   **KAREN:** I thought you wanted kids. You always tell me you do.

11   **BOBBY:** That's right, I *do*, but this is not what I had in mind.

12   **KAREN:** Oh, please, you're not going to give me that Norman

13   Rockwell scenario of the "perfect life" and the "perfect

14   woman" again, are you?

15   **BOBBY:** Excuse me, but I'll thank you not to dismiss my plan.

16   **KAREN:** You have had this plan since we were kids. Do you

17   remember that list you showed me for the "perfect woman"?

18   **BOBBY:** I was seventeen when I wrote that and it was a joke ...

19   mostly.

20   **KAREN:** I know, but the only difference on that list since then was

21   you added the rule, "Must never have slept with any barnyard

22   denizen."

23   **BOBBY:** Let's just forget that for now. Let me ask you one

24   question. Why me?

25   **KAREN:** Honestly?

26   **BOBBY:** Yes.

27   **KAREN:** Fine. *(Pause)* You are my best friend. We've known each

28   other most of our lives. There is no man that I care about or

29   respect more than you. You are kind, gentle, intelligent, and a

30   good person. Any child would be lucky to have you as a father.

31   **BOBBY:** Never in my life have I been so touched and horrified at

32   the same time. I think you've invented a new emotion ...

33   "touchified."

34   **KAREN:** Bob, I *want* your help!

35   **BOBBY:** *Stop saying that!*

1   KAREN: Not until you think about this seriously.
2   BOBBY: Don't you think this kid would be slightly screwed up
3   growing up this way? Our parents *were* married.
4   KAREN: Bobby, it's the twenty-first century. How many kids do
5   you know whose parents are still married?
6   BOBBY: Well, there's ... there's ... OK, how about those parents
7   we met at that place during that ... function?
8   KAREN: They got divorced last month.
9   BOBBY: Oh. OK, bad example, but what if —
10   KAREN: Bobby, we can't live our lives contemplating "ifs." What
11   would happen if you keep waiting and it never happens?
12   Won't you regret not taking the chance now?
13   BOBBY: Probably.
14   KAREN: So stop contemplating "ifs" and do something. *(BOBBY*
15   *stops and thinks.)*
16   BOBBY: OK ... I will think about it. But you have to give me time.
17   Now go home and let me think. *(KAREN gives BOBBY a hug.)*
18   KAREN: Thank you. You won't regret this.
19   BOBBY: Are you kidding? I already do. I'll talk to you in a couple
20   of days. *(KAREN starts to exit, but turns back.)*
21   KAREN: Bob?
22   BOBBY: What? No, don't tell me, you want twins now.
23   KAREN: No. I just wanted to say thanks and I love you.
24   BOBBY: You'd damn well better. *(She smiles and exits.)*
25   **The End**
26
27
28
29
30
31
32
33
34
35

14. The Stakeout

CAST: SCOTT, RON

SCENE OPENS: SCOTT is standing in front of a mirror. He is a cop. He is dressed to go out on a stakeout. Off-stage is his partner RON. He is also preparing to go out with SCOTT on the stakeout. They are yelling at each other.

RON: *(Off-stage)* **Scott!**

SCOTT: **What?**

RON: *(Off-stage)* **Forget it! I am not going through with this.**

SCOTT: **You don't have any choice.**

RON: *(Off-stage)***Wanna bet?**

SCOTT: **Would you stop complaining and get out here!**

RON: *(Off-stage) No!*

SCOTT: *Now! (RON enters. He is dressed as a woman, not an attractive one, but a woman nonetheless. SCOTT finds it hard to stifle his laughter.)* **You look ... beautiful.** *(He starts to laugh hard. RON starts to take off the wig.)*

RON: **That does it! I'm changing.**

SCOTT: **No, no. I'm sorry. It's just that I wasn't expecting — this.**

RON: **What did you think I was going to look like, a super model?**

SCOTT: **No, I wasn't expecting a super model, but I wasn't expecting Tug Boat Annie either.** *(SCOTT starts to laugh and RON throws his wig on the ground.)*

RON: **You think it's so funny — you wear the dress!**

SCOTT: **Come on, put the wig back on. We have to get to the park.**

RON: **Scott, why do we have to do this?**

SCOTT: **Because in this precinct all the detectives take turns on mugger patrol.**

RON: **Well, they didn't do this at my old precinct.**

SCOTT: **Hey, it's a real problem here and you wanted to transfer to where there was more action.**

RON: **Yeah. But I always assumed I'd get to wear pants.**

SCOTT: **Welcome to Manhattan South.**

1   RON: Great — so what's the routine?

2   SCOTT: Nothing too tough. We wait till dark and just walk around

3   the park waiting to be mugged. If anyone goes after you, the

4   purse or me, we get him. There's been a lot of problems by the

5   lake lately. That's where we'll be hanging out.

6   RON: OK, sounds good.

7   SCOTT: I just hope to God that nobody I know sees me with you.

8   RON: Why?

9   SCOTT: I've got a reputation for going out with some good-

10   looking ladies and you could shoot that all to hell.

11   RON: You know — you're not exactly my idea of the ideal date

12   either. And my girlfriend looked at me real strange when I

13   asked to borrow some eyeliner.

14   SCOTT: Speaking of which, you used too much.

15   RON: Who are you, Max Factor?

16   SCOTT: Fine, don't listen to me. It's your business if you want to

17   go around looking like a cheap whore.

18   RON: I thought that was the whole idea.

19   SCOTT: That's on hooker patrol. This is mugger patrol. There's a

20   subtle difference and you missed it.

21   RON: Great — now I have to redo my eyes.

22   SCOTT: I'm kidding. They look fine. But that dress —

23   RON: What about the dress?

24   SCOTT: It is way out of style.

25   RON: *(Getting annoyed)* Would you stop? I'm nervous about this.

26   SCOTT: Why?

27   RON: Never mind. You don't want to hear this.

28   SCOTT: Yeah — I do.

29   RON: OK — ever since I was a kid I wanted to be a cop. Then

30   when I became one out on Long Island, I realized I needed to

31   be one here, where I could really do something, so I

32   transferred. Now what am I doing? Playing a woman and

33   hoping I get mugged. I want to do well so I don't have to be

34   on mugger patrol forever.

35   SCOTT: Let me explain something to you. Everybody here does

1   this. Nobody particularly likes this work, but it's essential so
2   everyone takes their turn.
3   RON: I know. But I want to get into vice or homicide. How long
4   does that take?
5   SCOTT: Slow down. When you work here you have to walk before
6   you can run. This is probably the toughest city for vice,
7   homicide, and burglary cops. You just don't walk in here and
8   get those jobs. It takes a little time to see if you can cut it, or
9   even want to cut it.
10 RON: OK — so — how long does it take?
11 SCOTT: Depends on the man. There's no set formula. The captain
12   can usually tell. He's a good man. Want to know a secret?
13 RON: What?
14 SCOTT: When you came here the captain showed me your jacket
15   and asked if I wanted to partner with you. I said "sure." You
16   had an impressive record and that burglary ring you broke up
17   on the Island was good work.
18 RON: Thanks.
19 SCOTT: That scored some points with the captain.
20 RON: Really?
21 SCOTT: Why would I lie? Anyway, I don't think it'll be too long
22   before you're doing the work you want. Just be patient.
23 RON: OK — thanks.
24 SCOTT: No charge. *(RON puts his wig on, then a jacket.)*
25 RON: Well, I'm as ready as I'll ever be. You ready?
26 SCOTT: Yeah.
27 RON: Scott?
28 SCOTT: What?
29 RON: This is the first date. I hope you don't expect anything when
30   you bring me home.
31 SCOTT: Don't worry, any woman who'd wear those shoes with
32   that skirt isn't worth the effort.
33 RON: Hey — what's wrong with these shoes? You should've seen
34   the size of the woman I had to fight to get them …
35   The End

15. The Ballplayer

CAST: JANET, EDDIE

SCENE OPENS: We are in the living room of an apartment. Sitting on the couch is JANET. She is a pretty young woman in her twenties. She is an actress. She shares an apartment with her boyfriend, EDDIE. He is a pro ballplayer. Tall, blonde, and in his twenties. JANET is sort of reading a magazine, but is obviously very annoyed. EDDIE enters.

EDDIE: Janet, honey, I'm home.

JANET: Hoo-ray. *(Hurrah)*

EDDIE: What's the matter, Babe. I'm not late, am I? *(He sits next to her on the couch.)*

JANET: You're not?

EDDIE: No. You said to be home at seven o'clock and that's what time it is, see? *(He shows her his watch.)*

JANET: It's three hours slow. *(He looks at it.)*

EDDIE: It is? I guess it's still set on L.A. time. I forgot to set it back after that road trip with the Angels.

JANET: Didn't you think it was a little dark for seven o'clock?

EDDIE: Yeah, I did, now that you mention it.

JANET: We were supposed to have a romantic dinner for two tonight. I haven't seen you in the three weeks since you've been on the road with that damned ball team.

EDDIE: I said I was sorry. Can't we have dinner now?

JANET: The roast was ready two hours ago.

EDDIE: Can it be saved?

JANET: Sure. Why don't you save it and use it for second base tomorrow? *(She gets up.)*

EDDIE: I'm sorry. Practice ran late and then we had a meeting. How can I make it up to you?

JANET: Forget it. Let's talk. *(They sit.)* **When we first got together, you warned me that it wasn't easy being with a ballplayer and I said that I could handle it, but it's getting impossible.**

1   **EDDIE:** Why?

2   **JANET:** We never see each other. When we do, I've just come back

3   from a rehearsal and you're either coming or going to a game.

4   This is not what I call togetherness.

5   **EDDIE:** Fine, I'll give you all that, but from April till September —

6   or later — I'm a ballplayer. You knew that. It's my job. I'm

7   sorry if I have to go on the road, but that's the way it is.

8   **JANET:** OK, but when you *are* home, do you think you can make an

9   effort to stop thinking about baseball, at least for a little while?

10   Do you think that maybe you could pay *me* a little attention?

11   **EDDIE:** I always pay attention to you.

12   **JANET:** Who are you kidding? You don't even know that I'm alive.

13   **EDDIE:** That's not true. Just this morning I remember telling you

14   how great you smelled. *(Pause)* What was that perfume you

15   were wearing?

16   **JANET:** Glove oil. Your bottle fell off the closet shelf this morning

17   and hit me in the head.

18   **EDDIE:** Oh. No wonder you smelled like our first baseman.

19   **JANET:** See, that's all you think about.

20   **EDDIE:** Now, wait a minute, you're not a lot better.

21   **JANET:** What have I done?

22   **EDDIE:** Whenever you're involved in a play or movie, I'm never me.

23   **JANET:** What are you talking about?

24   **EDDIE:** When you did that Shakespeare play, I was Romeo for a

25   month. When you did *Oliver*, you kept calling me Fagin. And

26   last month, I never told you this, but I hated the name

27   Kowalski!

28   **JANET:** Well, I have to do something to get your attention. You

29   don't seem to want me.

30   **EDDIE:** That's not true.

31   **JANET:** Oh, yeah? You know, you're in great shape, but whenever

32   you're home, you seem to be on the "disabled list."

33   **EDDIE:** It's not that bad.

34   **JANET:** Yes, it is. I want my Eddie back. Do you remember how it

35   was when we first met?

1   EDDIE: How could I forget? You came to every home game,
2   waited outside the locker room, wore a team jersey with my
3   number on it, and you *hated* baseball. How could I ignore
4   you?
5   JANET: See, but now I'm right under your nose and you don't see
6   me. *(Stops and thinks.)*
7   EDDIE: *(Pause)* Maybe you're right. Look, I'm sorry. I can't tell
8   you how much I miss you when I'm on the road and how
9   much I look forward to coming home to you.
10   JANET: I feel the same way.
11   EDDIE: I guess I just forgot to show you. I will make a real effort
12   from now on.
13   JANET: Really? *(EDDIE gives her a kiss.)*
14   EDDIE: Yeah. We're home for the next ten games. We'll spend all
15   my free time together. OK? *(JANET gets frisky.)*
16   JANET: Yeah. Why don't we start right now?
17   EDDIE: Can we wait a little while?
18   JANET: Why?
19   EDDIE: *Pride of the Yankees* is on TV and I never miss it. *(JANET*
20   *drops her head.)*
21   **The End**
22
23
24
25
26
27
28
29
30
31
32
33
34
35

16. The Will

CAST: #1, #2

SCENE OPENS: We are in #1's office. #1 is a lawyer. He/she is preparing for a meeting. There is a knock at the door.

#1: Come on in. *(#2 enters.)* **I'm glad you could make it. Sit down.**

#2: I got your message. It sounded kind of urgent.

#1: It is.

#2: What's up?

#1: It has to do with the reading of your father's will tomorrow.

#2: And?

#1: Well, I thought we ought to talk about his will before then.

#2: What's to talk about? I know what's in it.

#1: When's the last time you two ... discussed it?

#2: I don't know. Must have been four ... or ... five ... *(A horrible thought starts to dawn on #2)* **years ... no, wait. Do not tell me that he changed his will.**

#1: See, this is why I wanted to meet now. I didn't want there to be a scene tomorrow.

#2: Why would there be a scene? The only reason I can think of is that he changed his will and I got screwed. And if that's the case ... fix it.

#1: Look, I want you to stay calm. I'm talking to you in the capacity as your lawyer ...

#2: Don't! Just show me the paper. *(#1 takes out a document and gives it to #2. #2 looks it over and is shocked.)*

#1: See, it's not really that bad.

#2: Not that bad? *Not that bad?!* **I got fifty thousand dollars.**

#1: That's a lot of money.

#2: When my father died he was worth forty million. My mother's dead, I have no brothers or sisters, my father has no other blood relatives ... so what happened to the other thirty-nine million, nine hundred and fifty thousand dollars?

#1: That's ... a little hard to tell you.

1   #2: I don't care, but let me warn you ... if you say he gave it to
2   Shelley I'm going to reach down your throat and pull out your
3   larynx. Now, where — did — the money — go?!
4   #1: *(Pause)* He gave it to Shelley. *(#1 lunges across the desk as #2*
5   *jumps out of the way.)*
6   #2: *I'm gonna kill you!!*
7   #1: Why me? I'm just the lawyer.
8   #2: That's reason enough right there. But that aside, my father's
9   already dead and someone must die for this.
10   #1: Just get a grip on yourself and sit down! *(#1 and 2 both sit back*
11   *down.)*
12   #2: Why didn't you tell me this before?
13   #1: Because your father told me not to. I was bound by privilege.
14   He said that if Shelley wanted to give you more that was up to
15   her.
16   #2: Yeah, right. I've got a good picture of that. Well, there's got to
17   be something we can do.
18   #1: Fine. Tell me what. Everything was legal.
19   #2: *Contest the will!*
20   #1: Just like that? On what grounds?
21   #2: I don't know! Think of something.
22   #1: There's nothing. He said he really loved her.
23   #2: Oh, please. Since my mother died that man hit on everything
24   with a pulse between the ages of twenty and thirty. Now he
25   meets a woman three months ago, marries her two months
26   ago and drops forty million in her lap, and you find nothing
27   wrong with that?
28   #1: Thirty-nine million, nine hundred and fifty thousand dollars,
29   and it doesn't matter what I think. The courts won't find
30   anything wrong with it. They need something illegal. They're
31   kinda funny that way. *(#2 thinks for a second.)*
32   #2: OK ... how about if we say she coerced him?
33   #1: And you can prove this, of course. Proof is another thing
34   they're fussy about.
35   #2: Why else would a twenty-four-year-old marry a seventy-year-

1   old? Unless she was planning to take his money.

2   #1: So what?! Unless she did something illegal, they won't care *why*

3   she married him.

4   #2: OK, OK ... how's this? We tell the courts he was crazy.

5   #1: Here we go with that old proof thing again. What do you have?

6   #2: Do you know how they found him?

7   #1: Not really.

8   #2: They found him dead on the floor dressed in a Cub Scout

9   uniform.

10   #1: OK, but that really —

11   #2: Wait, it gets better. When questioned, Shelley said they were in

12   the middle of playing *his* favorite game, "Den mother and the

13   naughty scout." He was going for his merit badge in spankings

14   when he keeled over. What do you think of that?

15   #1: I didn't know they gave out a merit badge for that. Still, a

16   person's sexual proclivities are not a barometer of their

17   mental capacities.

18   #2: *(Pause)* What the hell did you just say?

19   #1: Just because your father was weird, doesn't make him crazy.

20   #2: This is a nightmare.

21   #1: When he met her I told you to make friends with her. I warned

22   you this might happen.

23   #2: You're a lawyer. Who listens to you?

24   #1: Well, you better listen now. He legally married her and legally

25   changed his will. If you go into court, it's going to look like the

26   greedy offspring versus the grieving widow.

27   #2: "Grieving widow," my butt. She knew exactly what she was

28   doing.

29   #1: Maybe, but she was his wife, and technically, *your* stepmother.

30   #2: My stepmother? Then what does that make me? Cinderella? So

31   now the evil stepmother dances off to the castle with forty

32   million bucks and I get locked in the basement?

33   #1: Pretty much, unless you can find yourself one good fairy

34   godmother.

35   #2: *(Pause)* No, wait! I've got something better. Remember that

1	slimy little weasel we hired to investigate that last woman he
2	wanted to marry?
3	#1: Was that the guy who couldn't come out in the daylight?
4	#2: Yeah. Call him. Get him to crawl up her ... past with a
5	microscope and find me something that I can bargain with.
6	#1: You mean blackmail with.
7	#2: Bargain, blackmail, what's the difference? I need something!
8	#1: You know, this could get really ugly.
9	#2: No, it's already ugly. What it'll get is *lethal* if that bimbo walks
10	away with my money.
11	#1: I've got to tell you, I'm against this. I think you should talk to
12	her and try and work something out.
13	#2: You mean, be honest with her?
14	#1: Yes. I know it's a novel approach, but let's be different.
15	#2: Only as a last resort. For right now, call the weasel. Oh, and see
16	if you can stall the reading of the will until we can get
17	something on her.
18	#1: I'll do my best. *(#2 gets up and starts to exit.)*
19	#2: Call me later and let me know what's up.
20	#1: Where will you be?
21	#2: My house.
22	#1: That's the place your father owned in the city, right?
23	#2: Yeah.
24	#1: Maybe you should sit down again. I knew there was something
25	I forgot to tell you ...
26	The End
27	
28	
29	
30	
31	
32	
33	
34	
35	

17. The Tutor

CAST: BOBBI, KENNY

SCENE OPENS: We are in a living room. Lying on the couch is
BOBBI NEWKIRK. She is seventeen years old and very pretty.
She is dressed in shorts and a T-shirt. Entering is KENNY
TYLER. He is about twenty-two, a college student who is
tutoring for extra money. He knocks.

KENNY: Anybody home?

BOBBI: Yeah, come on in. *(KENNY looks around.)*

KENNY: Hi, I'm sorry I'm late. I'm Kenny Tyler. I'm looking for
Roberta Newkirk. *(BOBBI sits up.)*

BOBBI: Hi, Kenny. Surprise!

KENNY: Oh, no. It's you.

BOBBI: That's a real nice greeting.

KENNY: It's probably more than you deserve.

BOBBI: Thanks a lot.

KENNY: You're welcome. Look, I was hired to tutor Roberta, so if
you're finished with your little surprise, could you go and get
your sister?

BOBBI: I don't have a sister. I'm Roberta.

KENNY: I thought your name was Bobbi.

BOBBI: That's my nickname. Nobody calls me Roberta except my
mother.

KENNY: And she's the one who called and hired me?

BOBBI: Right.

KENNY: Right. Well, now that we got that cleared up, I think I'll
be going.

BOBBI: Wait a minute. You can't leave yet. You just got here.

KENNY: Watch me. *(He starts to leave.)*

BOBBI: Oh, I see. You're still upset about last summer. *(This stops*
KENNY in his tracks. He goes back to her.)

KENNY: Why shouldn't I be? The last time I saw you, we were
kissing, you bolted, and I never saw you again.

1   BOBBI: Did you ever try and find me?

2   KENNY: Of course I tried to find you. I checked the phone book

3   and information. Then I remembered that we went to the

4   same college. So I asked a friend of mine in administration to

5   check on your address.

6   BOBBI: *(Getting nervous)* What did he say?

7   KENNY: He said that you were never enrolled at State.

8   BOBBI: Oh.

9   KENNY: Yeah, "oh." So I gave up. Now, after getting you out of my

10   system, I get a call from out of the blue from a lady who wants

11   me to tutor her ... *(A horrible realization hits)* ... her ...

12   BOBBI: Her what?

13   KENNY: Her *high school* daughter? *(Pause)* No wonder you

14   weren't registered at State. You're not in college. You're in ...

15   in ...

16   BOBBI: High school.

17   KENNY: Thank you. *(Pause)* How old are you?

18   BOBBI: Seventeen?

19   KENNY: I'm afraid to ask the next question. *(Pause)* Were you

20   seventeen last summer? *(BOBBI hesitates and shakes her head*

21   *"no." KENNY drops his briefcase.)*

22   BOBBI: You don't look so good. Can I get you anything?

23   KENNY: Yeah, a real good lawyer.

24   BOBBI: Come on, it's not that bad. I haven't told anyone about

25   you or last summer.

26   KENNY: Thanks, that's flattering.

27   BOBBI: Come here. Sit down. I can't believe you thought I

28   was nineteen. *(Pause)* You know, your coming here wasn't a

29   coincidence.

30   KENNY: I was beginning to suspect that. How did you find me?

31   BOBBI: Well, I was at my girlfriend's house and her sister goes to

32   State. I was reading her paper and I saw your ad. I told my

33   mother that I needed a tutor and she hired you.

34   KENNY: Now that you've told me the how, you want to continue

35   with the why?

1   **BOBBI:** The why is because I wanted to see you again. I felt that I
2   owed you an explanation.

3   **KENNY:** I'm not really sure I care to hear it.

4   **BOBBI:** But I really did want to see you again. See, I even wore the
5   outfit that you liked so much.

6   **KENNY:** I remember it.

7   **BOBBI:** *(Coyishly)* When I used to wear it you used to tell me I had
8   a great butt.

9   **KENNY:** When I said that, I thought your butt was three years
10   older. *(She gets up and sits on KENNY's lap and puts her arms*
11   *around his neck.)*

12   **BOBBI:** Does it really make that big a difference?

13   **KENNY:** Fine! Let's assume for a minute that everything was
14   above board and *legal*. That still doesn't explain what
15   happened last summer.

16   **BOBBI:** OK, I'll explain. You see, things were really great then. I
17   was having the best time of my life ...

18   **KENNY:** That seems like a good reason to run away.

19   **BOBBI:** Would you let me finish? Anyway, that night you said
20   something that scared me to death.

21   **KENNY:** What? What did I say?

22   **BOBBI:** You said, ... "I love you."

23   **KENNY:** Oh, stupid me! I guess you would have liked it better if I
24   had what? Said I hated you?

25   **BOBBI:** You don't understand. When you said that I got really
26   scared. I just did the first thing that came to mind. I needed
27   time to think about you and things and ... *(KENNY starts to*
28   *laugh.)* What's so funny?

29   **KENNY:** You are. It's all starting to make sense.

30   **BOBBI:** What is?

31   **KENNY:** The whole situation. As I see it, you decided to play adult
32   all summer. Do all those things you couldn't do during the rest
33   of the year. Then things got a little too adult for you and you
34   reverted back to a little girl. Only you forgot, you weren't the
35   only one involved. I was too, but you didn't care about that.

1   BOBBI: That's not true. I arranged to see you again.

2   KENNY: And what if you hadn't seen my ad in the paper?

3   BOBBI: We would have probably bumped into each other ...

4   eventually.

5   KENNY: And what would you have expected me to do. Just drop

6   to my knees and thank God that I found you? And if I did,

7   what guarantee would I have that you wouldn't just run off

8   again?

9   BOBBI: That's not fair.

10   KENNY: It sure is. *(He starts to exit.)*

11   BOBBI: You really don't want to see me again, do you?

12   KENNY: Not until you grow up. I don't mean years, because

13   you're a lot younger than seventeen.

14   BOBBI: You can't leave like this.

15   KENNY: Watch me. *(He exits.)*

16   **The End**

17

18

19

20

21

22

23

24

25

26

27

28

29

30

31

32

33

34

35

18. The Sister

CAST: KATHY, MICHAEL

SCENE OPENS: KATHY is sitting on the couch in her apartment. She is nineteen or twenty years old. She seems very upset. She looks at her watch. She is obviously waiting for someone. MICHAEL knocks and enters. He is disheveled. It is late night early morning.

MICHAEL: Hi, are you OK?

KATHY: What took you so long to get here?

MICHAEL: I'm sorry, I got here as soon as I could.

KATHY: I'm sorry. *(MICHAEL sits on the couch next to her.)*

MICHAEL: Sis, what happened?

KATHY: David and I broke up. *(MICHAEL puts his head back on the couch and covers his eyes.)*

MICHAEL: Oh, no, not again.

KATHY: What do you mean, "Not again"?

MICHAEL: What I mean is the way you sounded on the phone, I thought you were dying.

KATHY: I am — my heart's broken.

MICHAEL: Oh, please Kathy. It's three o'clock in the morning. It's much too late for melodrama.

KATHY: I'm not being melodramatic. This time it's serious.

MICHAEL: It was serious when Garry left, it was unbearable when you left Tom, and it was the ultimate tragedy with Bobby. I'm going home. *(He starts to leave. KATHY grabs his arm.)*

KATHY: No, please. I know I've been a pest before, but I really am upset. I haven't been able to sleep, I've been crying all night, and I ate an entire pint of Häagen Dazs.

MICHAEL: Chocolate-chocolate chip?

KATHY: Uh-huh.

MICHAEL: OK — so it's serious. *(He takes her back over to the couch and they sit down.)* Now — tell me what happened, but try and make the story shorter than *Gone with the Wind.*

KATHY: OK, see I met David on Monday.

1   MICHAEL: What Monday?

2   KATHY: This past Monday.

3   MICHAEL: Hold on a minute, you're this upset about a guy you

4   met two days ago?

5   KATHY: Why shouldn't I be? It was love.

6   MICHAEL: *Love?!* There hasn't been enough time for an indecent

7   affair.

8   KATHY: You just don't understand.

9   MICHAEL: Oh, I understand fine. I get a call at two o'clock in the

10   morning from my lunatic sister who wants me to console her

11   about the breakup of a forty-eight-hour fling.

12   KATHY: It wasn't a fling. It was a relationship.

13   MICHAEL: If you call two days a relationship, I'm afraid to ask

14   what you would call it if you went out for a week.

15   KATHY: *(Walks to other side of room.)* I should have known better

16   than to call you. You've never cared about me.

17   MICHAEL: You're crazy. You're my sister — I love you.

18   KATHY: Oh, yeah? Then how come you tried to drown me?

19   MICHAEL: What?

20   KATHY: You know what I mean.

21   MICHAEL: No, I don't. Refresh my memory.

22   KATHY: You pushed me into the pool and held my head under

23   water until I passed out. Mom had to pull me out.

24   MICHAEL: What happened was we were playing in the wading

25   pool. I dropped you in and poured a bucket of water on your

26   head. The only reason you choked is because you were

27   laughing so hard you swallowed some water.

28   KATHY: OK, what about the time you tied me up and left me

29   outside.

30   MICHAEL: *I was eight years old!* Children do those things.

31   KATHY: Yeah, well, those things stick with you.

32   MICHAEL: I was wrong when I said you were a lunatic. You're

33   certifiable!

34   KATHY: You don't care about me.

35   MICHAEL: *(Moving to KATHY)* I do! That's why I'm going to tell

1   you something I should have told you a long time ago.

2   KATHY: What's that?

3   MICHAEL: *Grow up!* Start taking care of yourself and leave me

4   alone. *(Silence)*

5   KATHY: Fine, why don't you leave?

6   MICHAEL: Kathy ... wait. Let's talk.

7   KATHY: Why? You've made yourself perfectly clear. *(MICHAEL*

8   *goes to the couch and sits.)*

9   MICHAEL: Come here and sit down. *(She hesitates, but does.)*

10   What I said didn't come out exactly like I meant.

11   KATHY: Well, what did you mean?

12   MICHAEL: Kath, I was so proud of you when you decided to leave

13   home and go out on your own, but since you've moved here

14   you've made me your parent. If you want to be on your own

15   you can't call me at every crisis. This is what you used to do to

16   get attention when you were little.

17   KATHY: *(Softly)* I know.

18   MICHAEL: You do?

19   KATHY: Yeah, but it's only because I'm so scared to be out on my

20   own. I'm afraid no one will care about me.

21   MICHAEL: That's silly. No matter what, you will always be my

22   sister and I'll always love you.

23   KATHY: Will you help me if I have a problem?

24   MICHAEL: Of course. Just make sure you really need help,

25   otherwise it will be like the "little boy who cried wolf." I won't

26   know when you really are in trouble.

27   KATHY: OK, I'll try. Michael?

28   MICHAEL: What?

29   KATHY: Can I call you if I need someone to talk to?

30   MICHAEL: No.

31   KATHY: What?!

32   MICHAEL: I'm just kidding. Call anytime, but try not to get

33   lonely at two o'clock.

34   KATHY: OK. *(Michael starts to exit.)* Mickey?

35   MICHAEL: What?

1   **KATHY:** I love you. *(MICHAEL goes over to her and they hug.)*
2   **The End**
3
4
5
6
7
8
9
10
11
12
13
14
15
16
17
18
19
20
21
22
23
24
25
26
27
28
29
30
31
32
33
34
35

19. The Withdrawal

CAST: #1, #2

SCENE OPENS: We are in an office. #1 is on the phone.

#1: Judy, that is so wonderful! *(Pause)* How much did he weigh? *(Pause)* Seven pounds, seven ounces. That's a nice size. What's his name? *(Pause)* Erazmuth. *(Pause)* Yes, that certainly is ... a name. Well, you give little ... Erazmuth, a big hug from all of his uncles and aunts here at the Sperm Center of L.A. And a special hug from that certain donor he'll never meet. *(Pause)* You bet. Bye. *(#1 hangs up.)* Erazmuth? Well, I guess it takes all types. *(#1 hits the intercom.)* Sally, will you send Mr./Mrs. Gibson in now. Thanks. *(The door opens. #2 peeks his/her head in and looks around. #1 spots this.)* Please, Mr./Mrs. Gibson come in. *(#2 barely comes in and stands by the door.)* You can come all the way in, you know. You can even sit in this chair. *(Pause)* I won't bite. *(#2 comes over and sits in the chair by the desk.)*

#2: I'm sorry. I'm just a little ...

#1: Nervous? Why are you nervous?

#2: I've never been in a place like this before. It's a little overwhelming.

#1: Really? That's odd. It's everyone's job here to make you as comfortable as possible.

#2: Oh, don't get me wrong, eveyone's been very nice. Maybe it's just that huge statue of a sperm in your waiting room. It's a little ... disconcerting.

#1: Actually, smaller versions of that statue are available for sale. They're very popular. Would you like one?

#2: No, no, that's OK. I'm not much of, uh ... an art lover.

#1: Well, if you change your mind ... So, what can we do for you?

#2: Well, my wife/husband and I want to have a baby and we need some ... help.

#1: I see. Do you have our questionnaire filled out?

1 #2: Yes, here you go. *(#2 hands #1 a clipboard. #1 looks it over.)*

2 #1: You seem to have left an answer blank.

3 #2: Which one?

4 #1: Why you came here. What the problem is.

5 #2: Is that really anyone else's business?

6 #1: We do need it for complete records. So, what is your/your

7   husband's problem?

8 #2: This is a little embarrassing

9 #1: Let me help. Do you/Does he have a low sperm count? Are

10   you/Is he sterile ... impotent ... not interested?

11 #2: I have/He has ... *(Fast)* a low sperm count.

12 #1: See, that wasn't so tough. *(#1 starts to fill out the form.)* OK, not

13   enough little soldiers to attack the fort. Good, now that we've

14   got that out of the way, let's pick you out some sperm. *(#1*

15   *walks over to a bookcase.)*

16 #2: You don't keep it in here, do you?!

17 #1: That's very funny. No, we just keep all the sperm we have

18   catalogued in these books.

19 #2: And how exactly does one catalogue sperm?

20 #1: Carefully.

21 #2: No, I mean, what's the criteria?

22 #1: A lot of things. First it's by education, then we break it down

23   into subgroups from there. This first book is high school

24   diploma and below, this one is college, this one is graduate

25   school, then — those people who are doctors, engineers,

26   architects, etcetera.

27 #2: How about lawyers?

28 #1: No. Lawyers are in a book all their own.

29 #2: Why?

30 #1: Because ... they're lawyers.

31 #2: Enough said. What are those last two? *(#1 goes to a binder.)*

32 #1: This one has sperm listing of people with IQs of one hundred fifty

33   and higher and this last one is college and professional athletes.

34   *(Pause)* Obviously intelligence is no factor with this group.

35 #2: Well, why don't we have a look at that high IQ book?

1   #1: *(Chuckles.)* I'm afraid it's not that easy.

2   #2: It's not?

3   #1: Goodness, no! That book is not for everyone. It's our special

4   sperm book and there's just not enough to go around.

5   Anyway, we keep you with the group that you're most

6   compatible with.

7   #2: And just how do you determine that?

8   #1: Several ways. *(#1 hands #2 a little cup.)* First we need you/your

9   husband to give us a sample. *(Pause)* A sperm sample that is.

10 #2: Thanks. I may not appear to be in your top book, but I was

11   pretty sure that's what you meant. *(#1 hands #2 a piece of*

12   *paper.)*

13 #1: And here are the instructions.

14 #2: For what?

15 #1: How to obtain the sample that we need.

16 #2: Oh, I'm pretty sure that won't be necessary.

17 #1: Fine, whatever. When that's done, we'll run some genetic tests

18   on the sample and try to match you with the correct book. *(#2*

19   *thinks a minute.)*

20 #2: Wait, I think I get it now. On my questionnaire it tells you my

21   wife/husband and I just went to college, so we get sperm from

22   that second book?

23 #1: Exactly! Then once we run the genetic tests, we'll find a

24   genetically close donor to you/your husband who's bright, but

25   not terribly intelligent, like you two, and you'll have a nice

26   middle class, bright, not terribly intelligent baby. So, how does

27   that sound?

28 #2: I'm not sure. Let me ask you a bright, but not terribly

29   intelligent question. *(Pause)* Have my wife/husband and I just

30   been incredibly insulted?

31 #1: Oh, no. I'm terribly sorry if it came off like that. It's just that

32   you two don't quite fit the criteria to receive our top sperm. In

33   the same way you don't fit the criteria of our bottom book.

34 #2: What's in that book? The dregs of society?

35 #1: Actually … politicians.

1 #2: What's the difference?

2 #1: Very little.

3 #2: Look, if we're going to pay for sperm, we just want to be sure
4   we're getting the best.

5 #1: Everyone feels that way, but to use our top book you or your
6   husband/wife would have had to win a Nobel Prize, an Oxford
7   Fellowship, a Pulitzer Prize ... a Grammy. Have you won any
8   of those?

9 #2: No, but —

10 #1: I'm sorry but our hands are tied. You didn't even go to
11   graduate school.

12 #2: Do you know why?

13 #1: No.

14 #2: Let me explain. My wife/husband and I met in college and
15   started a business. It did rather well. We didn't need graduate
16   school.

17 #1: I think it's very sweet that you have a Mom and Pop shop.
18   What do you do? Make homemade baby furniture? Have a
19   flower shop?

20 #2: Actually, we started a company called Comp-U-Corp.

21 #1: *(Pause) The* Comp-U-Corp?

22 #2: Is there another?

23 #1: That's the largest computer company in the U.S.

24 #2: Second, but we're working on it.

25 #1: You're multi-millionaires.

26 #2: I wouldn't say that ... because we're billionaires. So, when I
27   say we want the best, *we want the best!* Am I making myself
28   clear?

29 #1: Crystal. Why didn't you tell me this to begin with? We could
30   have saved a lot of time and just taken you to ... The Vault.

31 #2: What's in The Vault?

32 #1: That where we keep the "Golden Sperm."

33 #2: What's the Golden Sperm?

34 #1: Donald Trump, Ross Perot, Malcolm Forbes, a couple of
35   Middle Eastern kings. You know, your kind of people.

1   #2: **That sounds more like it. Let's have a look.** *(They both get up*
2   *and start towards the door. #1 stops #2.)*
3   #1: **You know Mr./Mrs. Gibson, I'd be honored if you and your**
4   **husband/wife would consider my/my husband's sperm. I/He**
5   **could give you some wonderful offspring.**
6   #2: **That's nice, but I'm not sure if you actually fit our group. Can**
7   **you get me a financial statement?**
8   #1: **Absolutely, and if you wait a minute I can give a sample to take**
9   **with you and have tested on your own.** *(They start to exit.)*
10 #2: **That's OK. Maybe just a nice calendar ... or letter opener**
11 **would be better.**
12 #1: **Whatever you say ...** *(They talk as they exit.)*
13   **The End**
14
15
16
17
18
19
20
21
22
23
24
25
26
27
28
29
30
31
32
33
34
35

20. Students

CAST: KELLEY, BRUCE

SCENE OPENS: We are in the teachers lounge of any typical high school. Seated at the table reading the paper is KELLEY. KELLEY is a teacher. He is presently on a break. We hear yelling from Off-stage. BRUCE enters. He is also a teacher at the school. He is obviously very upset about something.

BRUCE: *That's it! I have had it! I'm through! I quit! (KELLEY looks at his watch.)*

KELLEY: **You're twenty minutes late.** *(BRUCE looks over and sees who's there.)*

BRUCE: **What are you talking about?**

KELLEY: **Well, it's ten-thirty. You usually come in here and quit at ten-ten.**

BRUCE: **Don't, because I'm not in the mood!**

KELLEY: **What happened?**

BRUCE: **Nothing, I'm just fed up with being a teacher.**

KELLEY: **You're always fed up. What in particular happened today?**

BRUCE: **You really want to know?**

KELLEY: **Yeah.**

BRUCE: **You know that teacher's aide that's been working with me?**

KELLEY: **Yeah.**

BRUCE: **Well, I left the room to get some supplies and when I came back they had hidden her jacket.**

KELLEY: **So? Kids do that all the time.**

BRUCE: **But she was still in it at the time.**

KELLEY: **Well, have you found her?**

BRUCE: **Not yet. I gave them ten minutes to return her.**

KELLEY: **Bruce, when are you going to learn that kids will be kids?**

BRUCE: **Please Kelley, don't give me that. Besides I've come to the conclusion that these aren't kids.**

1   KELLEY: Really, what are they?

2   BRUCE: They're little demons who just haven't sprouted horns

3   and wings yet.

4   KELLEY: Bruce, I hate to say this, but maybe you're losing it.

5   BRUCE: *(Ignoring him)* And the worst is that boy.

6   KELLEY: Which boy?

7   BRUCE: I don't know … you know, the one with the … weird hair.

8   KELLEY: That narrows it down to about two hundred.

9   BRUCE: The one with the electric chair earring.

10   KELLEY: Michael Chain.

11   BRUCE: Yeah, that's him.

12   KELLEY: What about him?

13   BRUCE: *(Very seriously)* He's the Devil.

14   KELLEY: What?!

15   BRUCE: I know it sounds crazy, but look it up, read the Bible, see

16   *The Omen.* You'll know that I'm right.

17   KELLEY: Bruce, sit down before somebody locks you up. *(BRUCE*

18   *goes to the table and sits. He starts talking to himself and*

19   *KELLEY.)*

20   BRUCE: I don't know what's happening. It started out OK today,

21   then all this, and I think I'm starting to lose it and … *(BRUCE*

22   *puts his head in his hands and continues to mumble.)*

23   KELLEY: Bruce, get a grip on yourself. God, it's always so sad to

24   see the good ones lose it.

25   BRUCE: Kelley, I'm serious. I'm really thinking about quitting.

26   KELLEY: Oh, come on, what would you do if you didn't teach?

27   BRUCE: I don't know, something safe and quiet like working for

28   the bomb squad.

29   KELLEY: Bruce, do you remember the first day you came in here?

30   BRUCE: That's like asking Europeans if they remember the Black

31   Plague.

32   KELLEY: That aside, do you remember how you felt that day?

33   BRUCE: Yeah, terrified.

34   KELLEY: OK, true, but you were so excited to be a teacher.

35   BRUCE: You're joking.

1	KELLEY: I'm serious. Ask anyone who was here. They'll all tell
2	you. You went around telling anyone who would listen that
3	you were in the noblest of professions. To be perfectly honest,
4	you bored us all to death with that speech.
5	BRUCE: Maybe I was like that, but I sure don't feel that way
6	anymore.
7	KELLEY: Why?
8	BRUCE: When I was in school, I always thought of teaching good,
9	polite kids who were there and wanted to learn.
10	KELLEY: Were you planning on teaching in Fake Land?
11	BRUCE: Great, just what I need, jokes from a biology teacher.
12	KELLEY: Hey, we're funny people. *(Pause)* Look, why don't you
13	be honest with me?
14	BRUCE: What are you talking about?
15	KELLEY: Why don't you just tell me that teaching wasn't
16	everything you thought it was going to be, and you can't
17	take it.
18	BRUCE: That's not true. I've been trying for three years.
19	KELLEY: Three whole years! Wow!
20	BRUCE: What's that suppose to mean?
21	KELLEY: It means that three years is nothing. That's not even
22	enough time for you to learn the ropes. Why don't you admit
23	that you're a quitter?
24	BRUCE: *I'm no quitter!*
25	KELLEY: Then what do you call someone who bails out when
26	things get tough?
27	BRUCE: Who's bailing out?
28	KELLEY: Is there anyone else here? I know I wasn't thinking of
29	quitting, so by process of elimination it must be you.
30	BRUCE: Nobody calls me a quitter.
31	KELLEY: What are you going to do about it? *(BRUCE is getting*
32	*very angry.)*
33	BRUCE: Don't worry, I'll think of something.
34	KELLEY: Something. You've sure convinced me.
35	BRUCE: OK, I'll prove it.

1   KELLEY: How?

2   BRUCE: I'll go back into that room and teach those kids if it kills

3   me.

4   KELLEY: Talk is cheap.

5   BRUCE: Yeah?

6   KELLEY: Yeah.

7   BRUCE: Shows what you know.

8   KELLEY: Then do it, prove me wrong.

9   BRUCE: I'm way ahead of you. *(BRUCE gets up, storms out the door*

10   *talking to himself.)* Who does he think he is … I'll show him a

11   quitter … those kids'll learn like they've never learned …

12   *(KELLEY watches him go, then picks up his paper starts to read*

13   *and says to himself:)*

14   KELLEY: This gets easier every time.

15   **The End**

16

17

18

19

20

21

22

23

24

25

26

27

28

29

30

31

32

33

34

35

Section Two
Drama

21. The Confrontation

CAST: JENNY, PAM

SCENE OPENS: We are in JENNY's apartment. She is a woman in her twenties. She has just brought her friend PAM back. PAM is banged up, with a broken arm. JENNY has picked her up at the hospital. PAM was in a car accident because she was driving drunk. This is not a one-time thing. PAM is an alcoholic. JENNY locks the door.

JENNY: The door's locked. Looks like we're here for the long haul.

PAM: Please, Jenny. I'm in no mood. We'll talk later.

JENNY: You may be dead later.

PAM: Jen, we're all going to be dead later.

JENNY: So you just decided to get a jump on the rest of us.

PAM: Please. *(PAM gets up and walks over to the window and just stares out. She talks to JENNY but doesn't look at her.)*

JENNY: I talked to your husband.

PAM: I had a feeling you might. So, you know all about me.

JENNY: Yes. Pam, you can at least tell me why you started drinking like this.

PAM: Do you remember that song?

JENNY: What song?

PAM: The one that went "Rain, rain go away."

JENNY: Yeah, so? What's that got to do with anything?

PAM: Well, it was a couple of years ago and I was at home one afternoon. It was raining like it is now. Anyway, I was alone, Rick was at work, and my mood was just like the day. So, *(Pause)* I had a drink, which I usually didn't do, and guess what? The rain went away. *(PAM turns away from the window and back to JENNY.)* Now I can make the rain go away anytime I want.

JENNY: The main problem with that is, the rest of that song goes, "Rain, rain go away, *come again another day.*" You don't make the rain go away, you just postpone it for awhile.

PAM: Yeah, but if you postpone it enough, you forget about it.

1   JENNY: So you plan to go through the rest of your life in a fog,
2   chasing the rain away?
3   PAM: Why not?
4   JENNY: I can't believe you're saying this. Pam, what happened to
5   you? You were always such a go-getter.
6   PAM: Try getting married right out of high school.
7   JENNY: I thought you wanted to marry Rick?
8   PAM: I did, but not then. My parents pushed me into it. You know
9   how they were. Old fashioned. They wanted me taken care of.
10   JENNY: You weren't happy?
11   PAM: Don't get me wrong, I loved Rick and I still do, but for years
12   I've been watching my friends, new and *(Indicating JENNY)*
13   old succeed and make something of themselves. You know
14   what I was doing?
15   JENNY: What?
16   PAM: Nothing!
17   JENNY: That's your excuse for being an alcoholic?
18   PAM: I am not an alcoholic. *(JENNY grabs her by the arm and takes*
19   *her to the mirror. She makes her look at herself.)*
20   JENNY: Then what do you call that? *(PAM takes a look at herself.*
21   *She touches her arm and bandaged face. She turns to JENNY and*
22   *starts crying.)*
23   PAM: Unhappy. *(JENNY hugs PAM as she cries. She takes her over to*
24   *the couch.)*
25   JENNY: Pam, what do you want to do with yourself?
26   PAM: Anything. I love my husband, but I want a life of my own too.
27   JENNY: You won't find it at the bottom of a glass or bottle.
28   PAM: I know that.
29   JENNY: You could have fooled me. Pam, you're young and bright.
30   You can go back to school, learn whatever you want, do
31   whatever you want.
32   PAM: I'm too old. I'd be embarrassed.
33   JENNY: It's that kind of thinking that makes alcohol your best friend.
34   PAM: You're not real sensitive, are you?
35   JENNY: I can't afford to be. You're my best friend and I love you.

1   I don't want to see you kill yourself.

2   PAM: Will you stop saying that? It's not that bad.

3   JENNY: Why don't you wake up? You almost did it tonight. You

4   need help.

5   PAM: What? A clinic? AA?

6   JENNY: Yes.

7   PAM: Jenny, I can't.

8   JENNY: Well, you better. I can help you, your husband can help

9   you, your parents can help you, but the most important one to

10   help you is you. You know what your husband said to me on

11   the phone?

12   PAM: What?

13   JENNY: He said that he loves you very much. He wants you to be

14   happy.

15   PAM: Then why isn't he here?

16   JENNY: Because he knows that you have to take the first step by

17   yourself. I don't mean that you'll be alone. He is there for you

18   and so am I, but the first step has got to be yours.

19   PAM: I'm afraid. *(JENNY hugs her.)*

20   JENNY: I know you are, and you should be, but I also know that

21   this is the best thing for you. I think you know it too.

22   PAM: If I do this, what happens after?

23   JENNY: That's up to you, but just remember, you can do anything

24   you want. That includes beating this. *(JENNY gets up and gets*

25   *some pamphlets. She takes them over and gives them to her.)* Why

26   don't you look at these? I'll make some coffee. *(JENNY gets up*

27   *and heads for the kitchen. She stops near the door and watches*

28   *PAM. PAM looks over the pamphlets, then slowly gets up and goes*

29   *to the mirror. She looks in and gently touches her face. She then*

30   *goes over to the phone. She looks at it for a while, then slowly*

31   *picks it up and dials. She clears her throat.)*

32   PAM: Yes, hello. *(Pause)* My name is Pam ...

33   **The End**

34

35

22. The Diagnosis

CAST: #1, #2

SCENE OPENS: We are in the doctor's lounge of a hospital. #1, a
resident, is at a table going over a file. #2, a doctor, enters and gets
some coffee.

#2: Hey, I thought you were off a couple of hours ago.

#1: I was.

#2: Then go home. You've just finished a thirty-six hour shift.

#1: Soon. I'm still going over a case. *(#2 sits at the table next to #1.)*

#2: Tell me about it.

#1: I have a juvenile male, five years old, who came in with
multiple bruises ...

#2: Do you suspect abuse?

#1: No, not at all. The parents are friends of mine and they pointed
the bruises out. They said he seemed to bruise very easily.

#2: That doesn't mean it can't be abuse.

#1: I took a look at them. The bruise pattern didn't fit abuse. Also,
several of the bruises looked like Petechiae. *(Pet — Tiki — I)*

#2: Really? Did the child have any other symptoms?

#1: Chronic fatigue, unexplained fevers.

#2: Any bone or joint pain?

#1: Uh-huh. So, I did a blood count.

#2: And?

#1: Well, the white cell count was somewhat elevated, but not
extremely high.

#2: Was he anemic?

#1: Severely.

#2: Not good. How did you proceed?

#1: How do you think? I did a bone marrow biopsy.

#2: And those are the results you're waiting for?

#1: Yes.

#2: You want me to call and see if I can get them for you?

#1: No need. *(#1 hands #2 a folder. #2 opens it and scans the lab*

1   *results. #2 starts shaking his/her head.)*
2   #2: This is one sick little boy. Have you told his parents yet?
3   #1: No, I just got the results back. But ...
4   #2: But, what?
5   #1: I don't know if I *can* tell them.
6   #2: "I don't know if I can tell them"? This is not a debatable
7   question.
8   #1: It's also not that easy. This little boy is not just any patient. He's
9   got a name. David. And I know him and his parents.
10 #2: And the disease he's got has a name. Acute Lymphoblastic
11   Leukemia. You know it and David's parents have to be
12   informed.
13 #1: I can't tell these parents that their little boy is going to die.
14 #2: These test results don't say conclusively that he's going to die.
15 #1: Come on, I don't even have to stage it to know that we didn't
16   catch it early. *(#1 gets very quiet and sits back.)*
17 #2: What's this really about?
18 #1: How can I tell *these* people their son may die?
19 #2: You do it in your best professional manner. Explain what the
20   options are, what we —
21 #1: No, you don't understand. These people are my friends. That's
22   why they brought David to me. They know me and they trust
23   me. I can't give them news like this. I just get the feeling
24   that ... I've let them down.
25 #2: Why? Because their little boy has a problem that they weren't
26   expecting? I have a lot of friends who come to me and it
27   always seems that they assume that because they're friends
28   with a doctor, they have some ... exemption from disease.
29   Your friends probably feel the same way. *(Pause)* I wish it
30   were true.
31 #1: But why these people and this little boy? I held him an hour
32   after he was born. Just tell me why it has to be this child?!
33 #2: I could answer that if I were God, but I'm not ... and neither
34   are you. We're just doctors. What we're dealing with is a
35   disease. They just work the way they work. Cancer cells don't

1 **go out and pick this person over that because they don't like**
2 **them.**
3 **#1:** **It just seems so — cruel.**
4 **#2:** **It has nothing to do with being cruel.**
5 **#1:** **You wouldn't say that if you had seen how scared David was**
6 **when he came in. You know what a needle biopsy is like.**
7 **#2:** **And it's going to get worse with the treatments he's going to**
8 **have to go through. You know that, don't you?**
9 **#1:** **Of course I do!** *(Pause)* **I hate this!**
10 **#2:** **Who doesn't? Let me give you a tip. My father told me two very**
11 **important rules from his experience when I first became a**
12 **doctor. Number one: People get diseases and sometimes they die.**
13 **#1:** **And the other?**
14 **#2:** **Doctors can't change rule number one.**
15 **#1:** **Great. If you'll wait a second I'll write that down so I won't**
16 **forget.**
17 **#2:** **You do know you're lashing out at the wrong person, don't**
18 **you?**
19 **#1:** **Look, I'm sorry. I'm thrown and I don't mean to take it out on**
20 **you …**
21 **#2:** **I wasn't talking about me. You're obviously upset with yourself.**
22 **Let it go. Do your job.**
23 **#1:** **That's a lot easier said than done.**
24 **#2:** **Maybe, but if you really want to help your friends now, you owe**
25 **it to them to be professional. Sure, they need you to be a**
26 **friend, but more importantly, they need you to be a doctor.**
27 **#1:** **And if I can't help David, I'll feel like a fake.**
28 **#2:** **You can only be a fake if you promise them something you can't**
29 **deliver.**
30 **#1:** **That's just it. I don't know what I can deliver.**
31 **#2:** **How about your knowledge, skill, and your compassion for**
32 **starters? Draw on your own strengths and the rest will take**
33 **care of itself.**
34 **#1:** **One way or another.**
35 **#2:** **The bottom line is, David will either survive this, or he won't —**

1   and his parents have to be prepared for both possibilities.

2 #1: And I've got to prepare them?

3 #2: Yes. You're a good doctor. Now go do your job. *(There is a*

4   *silence.)* Look do yourself a favor — go home and get some

5   rest. Clear your head and if you need any help with this

6   tomorrow ... you know where you can find me.

7 #1: Thanks.

8 #2: Not necessary. *(#1 gets up and exits.)*

9   **The End**

10

11

12

13

14

15

16

17

18

19

20

21

22

23

24

25

26

27

28

29

30

31

32

33

34

35

23. The Meeting

CAST: JANET, ALEX

SCENE OPENS: JANET is standing Center Stage. She is twenty-one and a dancer. She is about to go to rehearsal for a show. ALEX enters. He is a man of about twenty-eight. He is also in the show. ALEX crosses the stage in front of JANET. He looks at her. He can't seem to take his eyes off of her. He turns and walks backwards as he looks. Because he is not looking, he stumbles and falls on his butt. JANET watches all this.

JANET: Don't tell me. You're a dancer?

ALEX: What gave it away?

JANET: Nothing, it's just a hunch. *(ALEX gets up.)*

ALEX: Hi, my name is Alex.

JANET: Hi, I'm Jam.

ALEX: Jam?

JANET: Well, it's really Janet, but my friends call me Jam.

ALEX: OK — so you have an affinity for condiments? What do you call your mother, Mayonnaise?

JANET: I see. Not only are you graceful, but you're clever too. My initials spell Jam, OK?

ALEX: Sorry, just trying to make conversation. *(Pause)* Are you in the show?

JANET: Yeah, I'm a dancer.

ALEX: I knew it.

JANET: Yeah? How?

ALEX: It's the way you were standing.

JANET: And how's that?

ALEX: Well, sort of like this. *(He makes an attempt to stand in a dancer's second position, but does it awkwardly.)*

JANET: And you're *not* a dancer?

ALEX: Only in my dreams.

JANET: Are you in the show?

ALEX: Yeah. I'm one of the guest artists.

1 JANET: Who are you playing?

2 ALEX: I'm playing the part of Murray.

3 JANET: Really? Isn't that the lead?

4 ALEX: Second lead. The part of Roger is the main lead, but that's

5   not important.

6 JANET: Why?

7 ALEX: The money's the same. *(JANET laughs.)* Hey, I got you to

8   laugh. I finally did something right.

9 JANET: I'm sorry, it's just that we get a lot of guys coming down

10   here to do shows and they are always trying to pick up the

11   girls. I'm just on my guard.

12 ALEX: All the time?

13 JANET: Have to be. See, most of the guys come here and do shows for

14   six weeks and then just disappear. It doesn't pay to get involved.

15 ALEX: That's a little cynical, but I guess I see your point. Why do

16   you think all the guys just disappear?

17 JANET: I guess they don't want to travel all the way down here

18   from L.A. once they've finished their shows.

19 ALEX: All the way down? This isn't Mexico. It's Orange County.

20   It's only twenty-five miles.

21 JANET: Tell them that.

22 ALEX: So I guess you've heard all the pick-up lines before.

23 JANET: Let me put it this way, nothing has surprised me in a while.

24 ALEX: How about if I was to offer to bear your children?

25 JANET: Please, if I had a dime for every guy who offered that ...

26   *(ALEX thinks for a moment.)*

27 ALEX: Yeah, but I'm willing to have a C-section. *(JANET starts to*

28   *laugh.)*

29 JANET: You're nuts!

30 ALEX: I know, but it's part of my charm. How do you like me so far?

31 JANET: I don't know. *(Pause)* The jury's still out.

32 ALEX: Let me know when they reconvene.

33 JANET: Why?

34 ALEX: Because I'd like to ask you out and I want to know if I

35   stand a chance.

1   JANET: We just met!

2   ALEX: I know, but I've always gone on my first impressions and

3   besides, why play games? It's so much easier to be honest.

4   JANET: I agree, but I really don't date much.

5   ALEX: I find that hard to believe.

6   JANET: No, it's true. I don't think I've had a date in a … a year.

7   ALEX: *(Pause)* Popular, I see.

8   JANET: No. I just work all the time. I have a lot of friends and we go

9   out as a group. Besides, there's no rush. I'm only twenty-one.

10   ALEX: You're only twenty-one?

11   JANET: Yeah. How old did you think I was?

12   ALEX: Older.

13   JANET: How old are you?

14   ALEX: *(Pause)* Older.

15   JANET: Does this mean you withdraw your offer?

16   ALEX: No. I just have to rearrange my thinking.

17   JANET: Not really. I can stay out after ten o'clock and everything,

18   you know.

19   ALEX: Is that a yes, then?

20   JANET: I don't know. The jury's still out.

21   ALEX: God, I wish those suckers would hurry and get back in.

22   They're killing me here. *(JANET looks at her watch.)*

23   JANET: Hey, it's getting late. We'd better get in. Rehearsal's going

24   to start.

25   ALEX: Yeah. *(Pause)* Well, Jam, it's been a pleasure meeting you.

26   JANET: Same here. It should be interesting working with you.

27   ALEX: It will be. I promise.

28   JANET: Who knows? After six weeks I may take you up on the

29   child bearing idea of yours.

30   ALEX: Sounds good. Look, if the jury comes in before rehearsal is

31   over, want to get a bite after? That is, if you still eat.

32   JANET: We'll see. *(She exits. ALEX watches her go.)*

33   ALEX: It's going to be an interesting six weeks.

34   The End

35

24. The Sponsor

CAST: #1, #2

SCENE OPENS: We are in a diner or bar. #1 is sitting at a table. She/He has a drink sitting in front of him/her. #1 lifts the glass and looks at it.

#2: *(Off-stage)* **You don't want to do that.** *(#2 enters. #1 puts the glass down. #2 sits at the table.)* **Is that the first one you've ordered?**

#1: **I wouldn't have called you if it was the second. You'd be no fun to drink with.**

#2: **Let's put it aside.** *(#2 takes the glass and puts it out of the way.)* **Now we can talk.**

#1: **Why?**

#2: **Because that's how it works. See, as your sponsor, it's my job to come here and talk to you when you want to drink. It's not, however, my job to watch you stare at and possibly drink a glass of ...**

#1: **Scotch, straight up, no ice.** *(Pause)* **That used to be my favorite sentence. God, how I miss it.**

#2: **Tell me how this started.**

#1: **What's to tell? Life sucks!**

#2: **You wouldn't care to narrow that down a bit for me, would you?**

#1: **Sure. Pick a topic. Let's try relationships for two hundred, Alex. The answer is — he/she split for good. And what's the question? What did my girlfriend/boyfriend do today?**

#2: **Jeff/Janice left?**

#1: **That's another way to put it.**

#2: **Did he/she say why?**

#1: **Because I'm a drunk.**

#2: **He/She actually said that or is it what your inferring?**

#1: **What he/she said was that she/he didn't think that she/he could give me all the support I needed while I was in this healing**

1   period, and — how did she/he put it? — oh yeah, while I was

2   cleansing myself. Do you believe that? Makes me sound like a

3   self-cleaning oven.

4   #2: But you don't buy it.

5   #1: Of course not. I'm an alcoholic, not an imbecile.

6   #2: Why do you think he/she left then?

7   #1: I know why. I told his/her parents I was in AA at a dinner party

8   last month. Later I heard them tell Jeff/Janice that maybe I

9   wasn't the "right kind of person" for him/her to be involved

10   with if I had this kind of problem. It took a while, but he/she

11   obviously agreed.

12   #2: This can hardly be classified as a unique reaction.

13   #1: Well, thanks for that in-depth explanation.

14   #2: What do you want me to say? They're narrow-minded? — OK,

15   yes, they are. Maybe Jeff/Janice isn't quite the person you

16   thought? Probably not. It's still not a reason to drink.

17   #1: Then why don't we continue with my day? At work I was

18   informed that I'm still on probation and still not allowed to

19   handle any of my accounts alone.

20   #2: You seem surprised by that.

21   #1: You don't think I should be? I've been sober for six months.

22   Doesn't that account for anything?

23   #2: It counts for a lot, but answer me this: How long have you

24   worked for your present employer?

25   #1: Five years.

26   #2: How much of that time were you drinking? *(#1 doesn't answer.)*

27   Would "All of it, except the last six months" be factually

28   incorrect? *(Pause)* I didn't think so. Also, wasn't drinking the

29   reason you had to leave your last job?

30   #1: And your point is?

31   #2: You could have very well been fired from this job too. Instead

32   they not only let you, but helped you get yourself straight. If

33   they're a bit cautious, they have every right. You have to earn

34   the trust back.

35   #1: It was so much simpler before.

1   #2: Really? Can you honestly tell me that drinking ever helped
2   anything?
3   #1: Once, when I broke my leg skiing. My friend had a flask of
4   brandy and I drank the whole thing while we waited for the
5   ski patrol.
6   #2: So it numbed the pain?
7   #1: Hell, no! I had a compound fracture. It hurt like hell. I just
8   didn't care while I was drunk.
9   #2: Hold it! I think you may just found your own personal motto.
10   The number one reason you shouldn't drink.
11   #1: All I said was —
12   #2: All you said was, "I didn't care while I was drunk."
13   #1: I was talking about that one incident.
14   #2: Were you?
15   #1: Look, I don't want a lecture right now.
16   #2: Then why did you call me? You knew that's what I would do.
17   #1: I called because I needed a friend.
18   #2: Which one? Me or ... *(#2 grabs the drink and puts it back in front*
19   *of #1)* this? And if this is what you want, go ahead and drink
20   it. I'm not going to wrestle you for it. That's not how we do
21   things. This has to be your decision. *(#1 looks at the glass, then*
22   *at #2 and applauds.)*
23   #1: That was nice, very nice. Just the right amount of dramatic flair
24   to underscore your obvious and cliché-ridden point. Tell me,
25   though: Do you think the whole thing would have been as
26   effective if you didn't have the glass to punctuate your thought?
27   #2: I don't know. Do you know you're using an awful lot of words
28   to say absolutely nothing? I pose this question to you —
29   there's the glass. Are you going to drink it? And if you do, will
30   they trust you more at work? Will Jeff/Janice decide he/she
31   was wrong? Will anything be *any* better if you finish this? If
32   you finish five like this?!
33   #1: Your point is taken!
34   #2: Is it?! Is it really?!
35   #1: Yes it is! What more do you want me to say?

1   **#2:** I don't want you to *say* anything. I do, however, want you to
2   realize that people that have *never* had a drink have problems at
3   home and at work too. Everyone's life sucks once in a while.
4   **#1:** But I get to combine all that with trying to stay sober.
5   **#2:** Hey, you're an alcoholic and that's what you have to deal with
6   now. And believe it or not, you *are* winning.
7   **#1:** Really?
8   **#2:** Absolutely. You just can't see it, but every day you survive,
9   everyday you don't drink, is a victory.
10 **#1:** It's funny how winning didn't use to mean surviving.
11 **#2:** And the definition's going to keep changing. It's going to get
12   easier. You just have to believe that.
13 **#1:** Well, right now I don't believe it.
14 **#2:** What can I do to help you?
15 **#1:** I guess … what you're doing.
16 **#2:** Then that's what I'll do. Remember, you just have to take —
17   *(#1 stops #2.)*
18 **#1:** If you say, "take it one day at a time" I will knock you out of
19   that chair. I've just heard one to many clichés today, OK?
20   Don't push your luck.
21 **#2:** Fair enough. *(Pause)* You ready to go?
22 **#1:** I suppose. *(They both get up and get ready to leave.)*
23 **#2:** Did you pay for that drink?
24 **#1:** No, why should I? I didn't drink it.
25 **#2:** But you ordered it.
26 **#1:** Do you mean I have to pay for a drink I didn't get to have?
27 **#2:** Hey, like I said, sometimes life sucks. *(#1 leaves some money.)*
28 **#2:** Don't forget a tip. *(#1 leaves another dollar.)*
29 **#1:** Boy, this day keeps getting worse and worse. *(They exit.)*
30   **The End**
31
32
33
34
35

25. The Affair

CAST: #1, #2

SCENE OPENS: We are in a house. #1 enters having just gotten back from a business trip. #1 puts down a suitcase and coat and heads towards the back of the house. After a beat #1 returns very quickly, picking up the coat and suitcase. #2 enters, closing up a robe.

#2: Stop! Aren't you even going to wait for an explanation?

#1: You can explain this?

#2: It's not what you think.

#1: It's not? Tell me, when I walked in, were you in our bed with someone other than me?

#2: Yes, but ...

#1: It's exactly what I was thinking. *(#1 starts to exit.)*

#2: I didn't plan any of this. It just ... happened.

#1: I see. So the person in there is your insurance agent, right?

#2: Don't ...

#1: And you two were discussing a term life policy in the bedroom. You tripped fell on your agent, all your clothes fell off, you both landed on the bed, and I walked in at that precise moment. I can see how you wouldn't plan that.

#2: You want to keep your voice down?

#1: Why, so I won't make the naked person in my bed uncomfortable? How utterly inconsiderate of me.

#2: You know, it's this kind of attitude that got us in this position.

#1: *What?!* God, this is so you. I go on a business trip, you have an affair, and it's my fault.

#2: I didn't say it was your fault. It's *our* fault.

#1: Unless I was in bed with you two, it's not my fault at all.

#2: If everything was so great, do you think I'd be doing ... this?

#1: Fine, then tell me what I did wrong.

#2: There's not one thing that I can put my finger on. It's everything, our whole relationship. It's ...

#1: Oh, you are really good. You should be in politics. You get

1   caught with your hand in the cookie jar, say you want to

2   explain, blame me, then continue with an I-can't-explain

3   explanation. What comes next, the old "If you don't know, I'm

4   certainly not going to tell you" line?

5   #2: Will you let me finish? What I was saying was there's not just a

6   *simple* explanation. I wish I could pass it off as just a fling, but

7   I love you and I can't do that.

8   #1: You love me? You've got a really peculiar way of showing it. So

9   what are you saying? Are you in love with this person too?

10   #2: No.

11   #1: Then … why?

12   #2: You haven't sensed *any* tension between us lately?

13   #1: No, I haven't.

14   #2: Then *that's* the major problem.

15   #1: So you *are* blaming this on me.

16   #2: No, I'm not. I'm saying it's part of the problem. You've been so

17   wrapped up in yourself and business lately that nothing else

18   seems to matter, including us.

19   #1: Would you please give me a break? When have you ever been shy

20   about expressing yourself or your feelings? Especially to me.

21   #2: This case is different.

22   #1: No kidding! Cheating on me would definitely be in a category

23   all by itself.

24   #2: Forget that for a minute.

25   #1: That's a little difficult to do with that person in there.

26   #2: *Forget him/her!* This is about us! We're dying here and you

27   don't see it.

28   #1: We're not dying. You're killing us. And about as blatantly as

29   you could.

30   #2: OK, think about that. Does any of this make any sense to you?

31   #1: What?

32   #2: Me. Here, like this.

33   #1: I wouldn't have thought so, but now — I don't know.

34   #2: Well, let me clue you in. It's not me. Did it ever occur to you that

35   maybe I wanted to get caught?

1   #1: Well, congratulations, you did!

2   #2: Now ask yourself why.

3   #1: No, you *tell* me why!

4   #2: Because things aren't right between us anymore. Do you know
5   how long it's been since you've touched me? Everything in
6   your life is receiving some attention from you. Everything
7   except me, that is.

8   #1: OK, my work is getting most of my attention, I'll give you that,
9   but you were the one who told me that if I really wanted to get
10   ahead, I'd have to focus myself. Really push.

11 #2: Yeah, you pushed all right. You pushed me straight into bed
12   with another person. And it's not because I'm in love with
13   him/her. It's because I'm afraid that you're not in love with
14   me. I needed to feel wanted and I'm not getting it from you.
15   Not for a while now.

16 #1: Did you read that little speech in some book or hear it in some
17   movie, because it's crap and you know it.

18 #2: How can you say that?

19 #1: Because we've been through this before.

20 #2: When?

21 #1: When we first started living together. You were having a lot of
22   trouble at work and you told me you'd be distant for a while.

23 #2: It wasn't the same thing.

24 #1: It was exactly the same thing!! I also felt neglected for a long
25   time there. The difference is, I didn't go looking for attention.
26   I trusted you and us. And if you don't know what trust means,
27   look it up. You should know the definition considering you
28   obliterated it.

29 #2: So why didn't you ever talk to me then?

30 #1: Because things settled down for you, but if it had gone on any
31   longer, I would have.

32 #2: And how do I know that you've never cheated on me?

33 #1: Because I'm telling you I didn't. Unlike me, *you* have no reason
34   to believe I'd lie. *(Pause)* You know what's ironic? This trip
35   got me the promotion. On my way back I booked us on a two-

1   **week vacation, just you and me.** *(#2 loses all pretense.)*
2   **#2:** *(Pause)* **I'm sorry.**
3   **#1: Aren't we all?**
4   **#2: So … that's it. It's over?**
5   **#1: I wish I could say yes. God, I wish I could say yes, but the facts**
6   **are that I love you. I have never felt as betrayed and hurt as I**
7   **do, but I do love you.**
8   **#2: So where does that leave us?**
9   **#1: Well, I'm going on that trip. It'll give me time to think. I suggest**
10   **you do the same while I'm away.** *(#1 starts to exit.)*
11   **#2: Can … we be saved?**
12   **#1: I don't know. I honestly don't know.** *(#1 gets to the door and*
13   *turns back.)* **You'd better get back to your friend. He's/She's**
14   **probably lonely.** *(#1 exits.)*
15   **The End**
16
17
18
19
20
21
22
23
24
25
26
27
28
29
30
31
32
33
34
35

26. The Patsy

CAST: #1, #2

SCENE OPENS: We are in a police station. #1 is sitting at an interrogation table. He/She is visibly upset and extremely nervous. #2, a police detective, comes in. He/she goes to the table, throws a folder on the table, sits, stares at #1, and finally speaks.

#2: Well, if I'm not mistaken, and I'm not, apparently someone is in a whole peck of trouble, huh?

#1: You've made a mistake. I didn't do anything.

#2: Really? *(#2 opens the folder and reads.)* Let's see, you're Jeff/Jane Martin, right?

#1: Yes.

#2: You know a Mark Simpson.

#1: Barely. We hang out at the same club sometimes.

#2: Well, you obviously know him well enough to sell him some drugs. Cocaine to be exact. *(#1 starts to get upset.)*

#1: I don't know what you're talking about! That's nothing but a —

#2: Please spare me the song and dance. *(#2 pulls a picture out of the file and slides it over to #1.)* This was taken tonight at the Crush Club. That is you at the table with Mark, is it not?

#1: Well, ...

#2: Actually, that was a rhetorical question. We both know it is. And that little package that's sliding between you. That would be ...

#1: I have no idea. I —

#2: It's pretty high-grade coke. We've already had it tested. The picture's not bad either. I'll bet you didn't even notice the guy taking the picture at the next table. I gotta tell you — those digital cameras are amazing. So, now — you wanna cut the crap and tell me about it?

#1: I didn't know what it was. A friend of mine just asked me to give it to Mark. I was doing him a favor.

#2: So you gave a guy you "barely know" a wrapped package and asked no questions?

1   **#1: That's what happened.**

2   **#2: OK — you stick to that story. If nothing else, you'll give the**

3   **judge and jury a really good laugh.**

4   **#1: It's not a story, it's the truth.**

5   **#2: Look, Mark Simpson is an undercover cop. We've had the**

6   **Crush Club under surveillance for quite a while. Not to**

7   **mention some of it's ... patrons. So, if you're going to stick to**

8   **that ... story, you'll excuse me while I go talk to someone who**

9   **doesn't want to spend the somewhere in the neighborhood of**

10   **the next ten to twenty-five in jail. Have a nice day.** *(#2 gets up*

11   *and starts to leave.)*

12   **#1: I can't go to jail.**

13   **#2: Sure you can. See, you walk into court with the same B.S.**

14   **you're trying to pull here and ... going to jail is not going to be**

15   **a problem. Ever getting out again? Well, that's another story.**

16   **#1: But I didn't do anything!** *(#1 sits down again and slams down*

17   *his/her hand on the table.)*

18   **#2: I am going to give you one last chance to cut this crap and talk**

19   **to me.** *(Pause)* **Do you think we're really interested in** *you***?**

20   **Don't get me wrong — we will put you away, but we're much**

21   **more interested in the guy who's paying you.** *(Silence)*

22   **#1: I ... I don't know ... I mean, that ...**

23   **#2: Look — we know you're stupid, the question is — just how**

24   **stupid are you? Let me make this easier for you. How did meet**

25   **Jimmy Duncan?** *(#1 starts to answer.)* **And don't even think of**

26   **saying, "who" 'cause I'll bury you so deep they'll find Jimmy**

27   **Hoffa before you. Now — how did you meet Jimmy Duncan?**

28   **#1:** *(Pause)* **A friend introduced us.**

29   **#2: Glenn Carter?**

30   **#1: How did you know?**

31   **#2: We picked him up last night.**

32   **#1: Oh, God. Look, I can't say anything about Jimmy.**

33   **#2: Why? 'Cause he's such a good friend?**

34   **#1: No, it's just that he's threatened me. He said that if I ever open**

35   **my mouth he'll ... well, you know.**

1   #2: Yeah, I do and I guess that kinda goes with the territory. But
2   that doesn't make any difference. I want to know everything
3   you know about him. See, this guy is moving more product
4   around town than even *you* know. We want to know who's
5   supplying him.
6   #1: Hey, I never met anyone else. I swear it.
7   #2: And I believe you. But we gotta take these things one step at a
8   time. First you, then him, then — who knows?
9   #1: Look, I really don't know a lot. Really.
10   #2: Tell me what you do know. I'll judge what's important. *(#1*
11   *thinks.)*
12   #1: OK — I noticed that my friend Glenn had had a little more
13   money recently. When I asked him he said he was scoring
14   some easy cash by making some "deliveries" for a friend.
15   Then he asked me if I wanted to get in on it. First I said no,
16   but he told me how much he was making, so I couldn't resist.
17   #2: Where you'd meet Duncan?
18   #1: At the All Nighter Club.
19   #2: Really? I didn't think he did business there.
20   #1: I don't think he does. I don't think he goes to the clubs where
21   he — "delivers."
22   #2: Speaking of which — where does he give you your packages?
23   #1: He doesn't. Some big guy named Maxie …
24   #2: Maxie Swain?
25   #1: I don't know. I just know him as Maxie. Anyway, he calls me
26   and tells me where to meet him and he gives me my deliveries.
27   #2: When do you pay him?
28   #1: As soon as I can. That guy scares me. *(#1 leans back and ponders*
29   *this.)*
30   #2: OK — here's what I want to do. I want you to meet with him as
31   usual. Only this time you'll be wearing a wire.
32   #1: Are you nuts?! I'm not meeting him again! Especially with a
33   microphone on. What if he finds out? He'll kill me.
34   #2: Look, no one knows we picked you up. Did you call anyone yet?
35   #1: No.

1   #2: Then you're clear. You go, get your usual pick-up, and we'll do
2   the rest.
3   #1: And you don't think Maxie will put two and two together?
4   #2: Maxie Swain couldn't put two and two together using both
5   hands and his feet.
6   #1: But Jimmy Duncan can. And we both know that he'll be the
7   first person Maxie calls when you pick him up.
8   #2: You let us worry about Jimmy. Just do your part and maybe,
9   just maybe, you'll get out of this without any jail time.
10 #1: You know, I hear you talking, but I don't hear you guaranteeing
11   me no jail time with my body in one piece.
12 #2: That's 'cause I can only guarantee you we'll do the best we can.
13 #1: Well that ain't good enough. *(#2 gets upset.)*
14 #2: OK you listen to me. You've only got two ways to go here. You
15   do what we say, shut up and thank God we're giving you this
16   chance, or you can continue being a jerk, in which case I
17   promise you'll be going to jail and what happens there — well,
18   that's anybody's guess.
19 #1: Not really much of a choice, is there? If I do what you want, I
20   may get it from Jimmy out there.
21 #2: Like I told you — we will do the best that we can. Just
22   remember you were the moron who decided that selling drugs
23   was a good idea. And the bottom line is, it's not really my job
24   to give a crap about you. I'm not your parent. I've told you the
25   way things are. So now it's up to you. But let me give you one
26   little piece of advice — don't be an idiot. We're giving you a
27   chance to get your life back. Take it.
28 #1: I need to think. *(#2 gets up and starts to leave.)*
29 #2: Fine, I'll be back in five minutes. This offer's good till then.
30   Think fast. *(#2 exits.)*
31   **The End**
32
33
34
35

27. The Last Good-bye

CAST: JENNY, JIMMY

SCENE OPENS: We are in a run-down bar. JIMMY is sitting at a table nursing a drink. JENNY enters, sees JIMMY and walks up behind him. She stands over him for a second.

JENNY: You know, it's sad to see someone drinking alone. *(JIMMY turns and is taken aback, then composes himself.)*

JIMMY: I'm not drinking. It's club soda. I ...

JIMMY/JENNY: *(Together)* **... never drink when I'm flying.** *(JENNY sits down across from JIMMY. She takes his hand.)*

JIMMY: Jenny, what are you doing here?

JENNY: I love when you call me Jenny. Did I ever tell you that? Ever since I was a little girl, it's always been Jennifer. My parents, my relatives, all the kids at prep school. Only one person's ever called me Jenny.

JIMMY: That's because "Jennifer" doesn't fit you.

JENNY: I know a lot of people who'd disagree with you.

JIMMY: But I don't care about them. Only you. *(Pause)* **What are you doing here? You said ...**

JENNY: I said that I couldn't see you again. I know. But I had to.

JIMMY: Does that mean you've changed your mind?

JENNY: *(Pause)* **No.** *(Pause)* **I still can't go with you.** *(JIMMY lets her hand go and walks away.)*

JIMMY: Then why did you bother to come here at all?

JENNY: Jimmy, don't act like this.

JIMMY: How do you expect me to act? You know how I feel. Do you think this is fair?

JENNY: Maybe not, but it's not fair to me either. I love you.

JIMMY: But not enough to go with me.

JENNY: You know that's not true!

JIMMY: Do I? Are you coming with me, then? *(There is a silence.)* **Asked and answered.**

JENNY: Why are you trying to make me the villain?

1   JIMMY: I'm not.

2   JENNY: Yes, you are. You act like it's a simple question. A simple

3   decision.

4   JIMMY: I act that way because — it *is* simple.

5   JENNY: No, it's not! You can't boil it down to, if I go I love you, if

6   I don't go I don't love you. It's not black and white. There are

7   a lot of grays.

8   JIMMY: Look, where I come from when two people care about each

9   other and want to be together, they make an effort to do so.

10 JENNY: And you don't think I did?

11 JIMMY: Only up until your family met me and decided that ... I

12   wasn't good enough.

13 JENNY: That's not true, and they never came out and said that.

14 JIMMY: Jenny, I love you, but sometimes you're so naive. *(Pause)*

15   Do you remember that party in Paris?

16 JENNY: Of course I do.

17 JIMMY: I was out on the balcony, your father came out, handed

18   me a drink, then told me to stay away from you. Before I could

19   say anything, he handed me a check. He said it was for my

20   "troubles."

21 JENNY: I don't believe you. *(JIMMY reaches into his pocket, gets his*

22   *wallet, opens it and pulls out the check. He hands it to JENNY.*

23   *She stares at it with disbelief.)*

24 JIMMY: So when I say that things are that black and white, I'm

25   not making up the rules. I'm just following them.

26 JENNY: Why didn't you ever tell me this before?

27 JIMMY: Because I simply didn't care. I wasn't in love with your

28   family. Just you. *(JENNY walks away.)* I'm really not trying to

29   hurt you, Jen. I'm just being honest.

30 JENNY: You know, honesty's a funny thing. It has a way of being

31   painful all by itself — without help from anyone. *(Long pause)*

32   So — where are you off to tonight?

33 JIMMY: Well, we're off to London, then we take off for Morocco

34   tomorrow.

35 JENNY: *(Softly)* That's funny.

1 JIMMY: What is?
2 JENNY: It just seems that we fly to so many of the same parts of
3   the world ...
4 JIMMY: ... but travel in such completely different circles. I know.
5   I guess that's why we're ... *(He looks around)* here.
6 JENNY: When are you coming back?
7 JIMMY: Why? What difference could it possibly make?
8 JENNY: Can't you just answer the damn question? I wanna know,
9   'cause I wanna know.
10 JIMMY: I honestly don't know, Jenny. It may be in a week or six
11   months. I really haven't decided yet. Not meaning to be overly
12   dramatic, but I guess a lot of it depends on who needs a pilot
13   and which way the wind is blowing.
14 JENNY: Or how long you decide to run?
15 JIMMY: *(He laughs to himself.)* So this is how you're going to
16   handle it, huh? You can't deal with the fact that you're
17   walking away, so it all becomes about me running.
18 JENNY: Well, aren't you? You won't stay here and fight for me ...
19   *(She balls up the check she's still holding and throws it towards*
20   *him)* so instead — you're just taking off.
21 JIMMY: It's what I do. I've never claimed anything else. And you
22   know that about me. And as far as fighting for you, if I even
23   thought that I had a chance ...
24 JENNY: What — you wouldn't fly off at a moment's notice?
25 JIMMY: *(Pause)* No, I'd just have a real reason to come back. But
26   really, what difference does it all make? You told me that this
27   is not how you saw your life. *I'm* ... not how you saw your life.
28   Let's face it, Jenny, you're London and Paris, and Rome, and
29   New York ...
30 JENNY: You're all those places too.
31 JIMMY: True, but from the *front* of the plane. You're all those
32   places from the back with your feet up, cigarette in one hand
33   and champagne in the other. It's just who we are. And even if
34   you could cross that gap, you wouldn't. You'd never defy your
35   parents ...

1   JENNY: I have no choice. They're my family!

2   JIMMY: And I'm a great distraction. That is, I guess, until

3   someone acceptable comes along.

4   JENNY: You don't believe that.

5   JIMMY: I have to, Jen. I simply can't let my life end because you

6   won't be a part of it. *(Pause)* No matter how much I love you

7   — and how much you love me.

8   JENNY: It can't end like this, Jimmy, it just can't.

9   JIMMY: Sorry to tell you, it already did. I gotta go. *(He picks up a*

10   *bag and starts to head out. He turns back to her.)* I love you,

11   Jenny. I really do. I just hope you get everything you want —

12   or at least everything you're allowed to have. *(He exits. She*

13   *watches him.)*

14   JENNY: *(Very softly)* I love you, Jimmy.

15   **The End**

16

17

18

19

20

21

22

23

24

25

26

27

28

29

30

31

32

33

34

35

28. Loss

CAST: #1, #2

SCENE OPENS: We are in an office. #1 and #2 are at their desks. The
phone rings. #1 answers it.

#1: Graphic design. This is James/Janet. *(Pause)* **Yeah, he's/she's
here. Who can I say is calling?** *(Pause)* **Hold on.** *(#1 turns to
#2.)* **Hey, you've got a call. Line two.**

#2: Who is it?

#1: Your brother.

#2: Thanks. *(#2 picks up the phone.)* **Hey, Teddy, what's up?** *(Pause)*
What? *(Pause)* **Yeah, I …** *(Pause)* **OK, hold on. Are they sure?**
(Pause) **Yeah. I'll be over as soon as I can.** *(Pause)* **Have you
told them?** *(Pause)* **OK, don't panic. I'll go over with you.
How's Joey?** *(Pause)* **Yeah, I'm sure. OK, see you soon.**
(Pause) **I love you.** *(#2 starts to pack up for the day.)*

#1: Are you OK?

#2: No.

#1: What's up?

#2: Family problem.

#1: Can I do anything?

**#2: No. Look, I don't want to leave you with all this. I'll take the
Cheever file home and work on it later.**

#1: Whatever. Don't sweat it. *(#2 starts looking on his/her desk for
the file.)*

#2: Where's the file?! *Where's the damn Cheever file!*

#1: Whoa, you wanna take it easy? *(#2 sits.)* **Talk to me.**

#2: *(Pause)* **You know my brother Ted? You've met him a couple of
times.**

#1: Yeah.

#2: Well, he just got back from his doctor. *(Pause)* **He's got AIDS.**

#1: Are they sure?

**#2: Yeah, they're sure. This was the second test. He didn't even tell
me when he got the first results.**

1   #1: Is your brother ...

2   #2: What, gay? Why is that important?

3   #1: Well, they might know how he got it.

4   #2: What difference does it make how he got it? If I said he had

5   cancer, would anyone really care how he got *that*? But to

6   answer your question, yes, my brother's gay.

7   #1: Do your parents know he's sick?

8   #2: That's a story unto itself.

9   #1: Why?

10   #2: Because they don't even know he's gay.

11   #1: Why hasn't he told them?

12   #2: Let's just put it this way, my parents aren't the most —

13   "enlightened" people.

14   #1: I'm really sorry.

15   #2: Yeah, me too.

16   #1: I'm sure they'll be supportive.

17   #2: For Ted's sake, I hope so. What's funny is that they are always

18   after us both to settle down, get involved with someone. Ted

19   has been. He just couldn't ever tell them. Now, all at once they

20   have to be understanding, supportive and lose their

21   antiquated thinking.

22   #1: Do you really think they're going to abandon him now?

23   #2: *(Pause)* No, I don't.

24   #1: Also, a lot of people live a long time with this. It's not hopeless.

25   *(There is a silence. #2 gets very quiet.)* What are you thinking

26   about?

27   #2: I just remembered something.

28   #1: What?

29   #2: My brother and I were little kids and our parents took us to this

30   farm one summer. I remembered Ted and I running around

31   this field trying to catch fireflies. I think we were six and eight.

32   Just one insignificant summer night that happened a long time

33   ago, but it seems like yesterday. I can even smell the air.

34   #1: It's strange how certain memories just pop up at times like this.

35   #2: Yeah, it is. I remember that we were lying in the grass, with this

1   big jar of fireflies, blinking, between us. We were looking up

2   at the stars and trying to count them. Then Ted told me that

3   when he got big he was going to buy a farm like that one for

4   him and me so we could bring our kids in the summer.

5   #1: That's a nice memory.

6   #2: Yeah, it is, but that's never going to happen now, is it?

7   #1: Don't give up hope.

8   #2: That's easy for you to say. You've never been in this position.

9   #1: I haven't?

10   #2: When?

11   #1: When I was in college. I told you that my parents died when I

12   was a baby and I was raised by my grandmother.

13   #2: Yeah.

14   #1: Well, she was the best person I ever knew. She made sure that

15   I had everything and that I got to go to college. Anyway, my

16   freshman year, she started to get ... forgetful. Then it got

17   worse. Later she was diagnosed with Alzheimer's.

18   #2: That's rough. What happened?

19   #1: By my senior year she barely recognized anyone. She ... hell,

20   she was pretty much a child. She was this really strong,

21   vibrant person and I watched her deteriorate piece by piece.

22   So I know what you're going through.

23   #2: What did you do?

24   #1: Loved her a little more every day. I was just thankful for each

25   day she was around and didn't dwell on what was probably

26   inevitable.

27   #2: Is this your sage-type advice?

28   #1: No, it's just what I did. I also didn't give up hope. If there's one

29   thing that history teaches, it's that anything's possible.

30   #2: I'd love to believe that.

31   #1: Trust me, you will. You need to — for yourself and for your

32   brother.

33   #2: And what else can I do?

34   #1: Aside from being there for him? Nothing right now. If he knows

35   he can count on you, it'll make things a lot easier for him. It

1   **did for my grandmother.** *(There is a silence.)*

2 **#2: Well, I'd better get over there.** *(#2 gathers up his/her things and*

3   *starts to exit.)* **You know, this whole thing sucks!**

4 **#1: I know. Call me at home later.**

5 **#2: Sure.** *(#2 exits.)*

6   **The End**

7

8

9

10

11

12

13

14

15

16

17

18

19

20

21

22

23

24

25

26

27

28

29

30

31

32

33

34

35

29. The Split

CAST: ERIN, ROBERT

SCENE OPENS: We are in the apartment of ROBERT and ERIN. ERIN is packing some things into cartons. She looks at her watch, then out the door and resumes packing at what seems like a faster rate. ROBERT comes in and stops. He watches her for a few moments. She doesn't seem to see him.

ROBERT: Need some help? *(This startles ERIN. She stands and turns to him.)*

ERIN: You weren't suppose to be home for another hour.

ROBERT: By the looks of things, that's about all you need to finish. You want to tell me what's going on?

ERIN: Do you really have to ask?

ROBERT: I guess not. When did you decide this?

ERIN: Last night, when you refused to talk to me.

ROBERT: I didn't refuse to talk to you. I got home late and I was tired. I didn't want to fight.

ERIN: It wasn't just last night, Robert. It was just the last straw.

ROBERT: Why?

ERIN: Because you are always tired. We've had problems for a long time and last night I realized that they are never going to get better.

ROBERT: So you decided just to sneak off, huh?

ERIN: I'm not sneaking.

ROBERT: Then what do you call *(Indicating around)* this?

ERIN: Packing. I was going to wait till you got home before I left.

ROBERT: That's your story.

ERIN: That's the truth! *(He starts to take something out of her hand.)*

ROBERT: Why don't you just stop and let's sit down and talk.

ERIN: So, now you want to talk. Always when it's too late. Well forget it. Now I'm too tired.

ROBERT: So you're saying it's over? Just like that, five years down the tubes.

1   ERIN: It's not "just like that." You and I both know that it's been
2   over for a long time.
3   ROBERT: You don't even want to try, do you?
4   ERIN: What's the point?
5   ROBERT: Fine! Just remember, this wasn't my idea. *(ERIN laughs*
6   *softly to herself.)* And what's so funny?
7   ERIN: Nothing. I wasn't laughing.
8   ROBERT: Then what?
9   ERIN: You're starting to rationalize already. "It's not my idea."
10   Why don't you just share the blame instead of trying to
11   exonerate yourself?
12   ROBERT: I'm not. I just want you to know that this was not my
13   fault. *(Now ERIN starts to get mad.)*
14   ERIN: Fine, I was the only one married for the past five years. It's
15   all my fault. OK? Satisfied?
16   ROBERT: Please, stop trying to play the martyr.
17   ERIN: Well, what do you want me to say?
18   ROBERT: Try saying you'll try to work this marriage out with me.
19   ERIN: *What marriage?!* We haven't been married for two
20   years. Sure, we live in the same house, but we're not even
21   good roommates. Roommates at least talk to each other.
22   Face it, Robert, it's over. Let's just call it quits and cut our
23   losses.
24   ROBERT: I refuse to believe we're finished.
25   ERIN: Start!
26   ROBERT: Don't you love me? Did you ever love me?
27   ERIN: Yes, Robert. I did love you, but that was a long time ago —
28   and let's face it, you really don't love me anymore either.
29   ROBERT: Don't speak for me.
30   ERIN: Fine. Look, when we got married we were in love, but it
31   didn't last long. Maybe we weren't ready. We should have
32   never gotten married to begin with.
33   ROBERT: I think we were ready.
34   ERIN: Come on, Robert, we were in love with being in love. We
35   didn't plan anything out. What we took for being romantic

1   was just enthusiasm. It's not the same.

2   ROBERT: Weren't you ever happy?

3   ERIN: Yes. I'm not saying it was all bad.

4   ROBERT: Just most of it?

5   ERIN: Yeah, just most of it. If you really think about it, you'll

6   know I'm right. *(ROBERT sits and looks at her. There is a long*

7   *pause.)*

8   ROBERT: You're right. *(This was said very softly.)*

9   ERIN: What?

10   ROBERT: I said — you're right. *(She looks at him for a long time.)*

11   ERIN: Feels better to admit it, doesn't it?

12   ROBERT: Yes and no.

13   ERIN: Why yes and no?

14   ROBERT: Because I guess I've known it for a while, too, but it

15   makes me sad. You've been a part of my life for a long time.

16   Good and bad, but you've been there. It's not easy to give up

17   a part of your life.

18   ERIN: It may not be easy, but it's the healthy thing to do. Robert,

19   we've been friends since high school. We started out as good

20   friends. If we fooled ourselves and stayed married, we'd wind

21   up hating each other. True?

22   ROBERT: True.

23   ERIN: Maybe this way we can still at least stay friends.

24   ROBERT: Is that supposed to be a consolation?

25   ERIN: No. Just the best alternative. Think about it.

26   ROBERT: I don't have to, you're right.

27   ERIN: I am going to miss you.

28   ROBERT: Me too. So, where are you going?

29   ERIN: I'm staying with my sister until I find my own place.

30   ROBERT: You will let me know, won't you?

31   ERIN: Oh sure, sure. *(She starts to tear up as she looks around.)*

32   Well, I guess I should be going. *(She grabs a suitcase.)* I'll get

33   my other stuff tomorrow.

34   ROBERT: It'll be here. *(She heads for the door.)* Erin?

35   ERIN: Yeah?

1   **ROBERT: Stay in touch, huh?** *(She just looks at him for a while, then*
2   *heads out the door.)*
3   **The End**
4
5
6
7
8
9
10
11
12
13
14
15
16
17
18
19
20
21
22
23
24
25
26
27
28
29
30
31
32
33
34
35

30. Good-bye

CAST: #1, #2

SCENE OPENS: We are in a room. It could be a hospital or a hospice. #1 is at a bed unpacking a suitcase. From behind, #2 enters. #2 stands for a moment, just watching. #1 stops, sensing someone else is in the room. #1 turns and sees #2. They stare at each other for a moment.

#1: What are *you* doing here?

#2: I ... I wanted to see you.

#1: *(Pause)* You've seen me. Get out!

#2: What?

#1: I said, get out! Wasn't that clear enough or do you need directions?

#2: Look, I know it may be a little late for this, but I wanted you to know that I'm here for you.

#1: A *little* late? No, a "little late" is saying we'll meet for dinner at seven-thirty and showing up at eight. A "little late" is getting to a movie after it's started. What you are is *too* late!

#2: What do you want me to do?

#1: I told you, get out! *(#1 slams the suitcase shut. The two stare at each other. #2 turns and starts to head out.)* You will never know how badly you hurt me. *(#2 whirls on #1.)*

#2: Damn it! *Why do you think I'm here?!*

#1: I don't know. To ease some of your guilt, I suppose.

#2: I'm not trying to ease anything. When I heard you were coming ... here, I thought you might need me.

#1: A year ago I needed you. Six months ago I needed you. Thirty seconds ago I still thought I needed you, but ... I was wrong.

#2: Will it make any difference if I tell you I'm sorry? *(#1 goes back to unpacking.)* Look, you have no idea what I've gone through in the last year. When you called and told me you were ... when you told me, I just couldn't handle it.

#1: Well thanks for clearing that up! How selfish of me. If I had

1   known that my dying was going to be such a burden on *you*,

2   why, I would have just avoided the whole thing.

3   #2: That's not what I meant. What I was ...

4   #1: You know, you *still* can't even say it.

5   #2: What?

6   #1: You said, "When you told me you were ... " When I told you I

7   was ... what? What?! *(No response.)* I'm dying! I have a

8   disease and I'm going to die. Probably in the very near future

9   and you couldn't give a damn!

10   #2: That's not true.

11   #1: Isn't it? *(Pause)* What, you think it was a picnic for me? When

12   they told me, it was like the whole world stopped. I felt like I

13   was walking through a wax museum. Everything looked real,

14   but nothing moved. When I got home I called three people —

15   my parents and you. At least I got support from two out of

16   three. But you know what? You were the first one I called

17   because aside from everything, you were my best friend.

18   #2: That's not fair!

19   #1: I'm dying. I don't have to be.

20   #2: OK, I know I let you down, but it wasn't because I didn't care.

21   The fact is — I care too much.

22   #1: Oh, you are good. I'll bet that after a year you even have

23   yourself believing that.

24   #2: It's the truth! *Yes*, I screwed up because I didn't know what to

25   say or do. We've known each other all our lives, but I didn't

26   know what you expected of me, and I didn't know if I could

27   deliver what you needed.

28   #1: I didn't expect anything, and all I needed was for you to be

29   there.

30   #2: I ... couldn't do that.

31   #1: Obviously.

32   #2: Because I couldn't sit and watch you die, smile and pretend that

33   everything was all right. I couldn't lie and tell you they might

34   find a cure and talk about a nonexistent future. Is that what

35   you wanted?

1   **#1:** **No! But how about having dinner with me? Or letting me cry**

2   **when I was scared, or maybe just getting drunk together?**

3   *(Pause)* **We have been through so much together. Couldn't you**

4   **have at least helped me die?** *(Silence.)*

5   **#2:** *(Softly)* **I don't want you to die.** *(#2 starts to cry.)*

6   **#1:** **I've got news for you, it's not the top of my "To Do" list either.**

7   *(They hug.)*

8   **#2:** **I'm so sorry**

9   **#1:** **Yeah — me too.**

10   **The End**

11

12

13

14

15

16

17

18

19

20

21

22

23

24

25

26

27

28

29

30

31

32

33

34

35

31. The New Boss

CAST: #1, #2

SCENE OPENS: We are in an office. #1 is sitting at his/her desk reading the paper. After a minute he/she puts the paper down and picks up the phone.

#1: *(Into the phone)* **OK, you can send him/her in now.** *(#1 hangs up and straightens himself/herself out. #2 enters.)* **Hey, thanks for stopping in. I hope you weren't waiting too long.**

#2: **Only about twenty minutes.**

#1: **Sorry, couldn't be helped. I was on a call to England. Just couldn't get off.**

#2: **That happens. So — what do you need?**

#1: **Sit down. I wanted to talk.** *(#2 sits.)* **I'm trying to meet with everyone since I was promoted to V.P. of Production.**

#2: **Jack/Jane, we've been working together for awhile now …**

#1: **I know, I just wanted everyone to know what they can expect of me … and what I'm going to expect of them now that I'm … well, in charge here.**

#2: **OK.**

#1: **Tell me, what are you working on now?**

#2: **Pretty much the same thing that I was when we were in the same office. You know, the Wilson Project, the Miller Deal, the Kramer Project …**

#1: **OK, I see. So — here's what we're going to do. I'm taking Wilson, Miller and Kramer away from you and giving them to some others to work on …**

#2: **Wait a minute; I've been working on these projects for months. You just can't do that.**

#1: **Actually, not only can I do it — I just did.**

#2: **Why?**

#1: **I think you're just a little … overloaded. I wanted to lighten your load.**

#2: **Lighten? That is my load. If you take those away — what the**

1   hell *am* I going to work on?

2 #1: The thinking was that — you should work with research for a

3   while.

4 #2: Research?! That's entry-level.

5 #1: Technically, yeah, but all those kids coming in need *someone* to

6   show them the ropes and who better than you?

7 #2: And just how *long* am I supposed to show them the ropes?

8 #1: I guess until I say otherwise.

9 #2: This is a bunch of crap, Jane/Jack, and you know it.

10 #1: You can call it what you want, but I am in charge here and I've

11   decided that this is where I want you. Now, you don't have to

12   do as I say if you don't want to. I can certainly arrange a very

13   nice severance package if you like, but believe me when I say

14   that your days as a project manager are done.

15 #2: We'll just see about that. *(#2 gets up.)*

16 #1: Have a nice day, Nick/Nancy. *(#2 starts to exit, but stops at the*

17   *door, turns and heads back to the desk.)*

18 #1: You having trouble finding your way out?

19 #2: Why are you doing this?

20 #1: I have my reasons. *(#1 picks up a pen and starts to write*

21   *something. #2 grabs it out of his/her hand and throws it across*

22   *the room.)*

23 #2: And you're going to tell me. You and I both know I'm the best

24   project manager here. *(#1 sits back and looks at #2.)*

25 #1: *(Pause)* Exactly and that's why I just can't allow you to do it

26   any more.

27 #2: What does that ... *(#2 gets it.)* I see. It *is* the promotion. You *did*

28   hear the story.

29 #1: What story?

30 #2: That the majority of the board wanted me to have this job, but

31   your dad decided to give it to you.

32 #1: Of course I heard it. I've been hearing them praise you since

33   the day you got here.

34 #2: And it's my fault that I'm good at this job and you — weren't?

35 #1: So, not mincing any word now, I see.

1 **#2:** What's the point? Apparently I've got nothing to lose. *(Pause)*
2   You're scared to death of me, aren't you?
3 **#1:** Don't flatter yourself. Annoyed, irritated, fed-up, maybe, but
4   not scared. I knew sooner or later I'd be getting this job —
5   you just made it later.
6 **#2:** But you got it. So why mess with me now?
7 **#1:** Because I plan to skate through this job until my father decides
8   to retire or dies and the last thing I need is for you to be
9   around. I also don't need any more comparisons or any little
10   birdies whispering in my father's ear about what an asset you
11   are and where your best place might be. Let's just call what
12   I'm doing — a little preventive medicine.
13 **#2:** And you don't think your father will be able to figure any of
14   this out for himself?
15 **#1:** Let me put it this way — my father's not exactly what I'd call —
16   bright. Not to mention the fact that he *does* have this soft spot
17   for me. So, no, I don't think he'll notice on his own, *but* ...
18 **#2:** ... but putting me outta sight or getting me to quit should make
19   sure of that.
20 **#1:** Exactly! Just like I said, preventative medicine.
21 **#2:** Wait a minute — this the same thing that happened to Tim
22   Johnson and Shelley Minter.
23 **#1:** Tim was pretty easy. He was new and not that well known. Now
24   Shelley on the other hand — that took a bit more finesse.
25 **#2:** You started that rumor, didn't you?
26 **#1:** I may have said something to someone, but after that, it really
27   took on a life of its own.
28 **#2:** So you just destroyed her life so you'd look better?
29 **#1:** Oh, don't get so melodramatic. What did I destroy? I heard
30   she's doing real well at her new company. So what's the harm?
31 **#2:** If you have to ask that question you're even more repulsive
32   than I thought.
33 **#1:** Look, I'd love to sit here all day and let you call me names while
34   I laugh in your face, but I do have to at least appear to be
35   doing my job and you — well, you have to get to research or

1   — the unemployment line, which ever you want.
2   #2: You're never going to get away with this.
3   #1: Spoken in true movie fashion. But as a punctuation to this
4   whole conversation, look around. Not only will I get away
5   with this, I apparently already have.
6   #2: And what makes you think I won't go right to your father?
7   #1: And tell him what? He knows you were up for this job and if
8   you go in spouting all these fantastic stories about me, what do
9   you think he's going to do? Fire me? Hell, he won't even
10   believe you. You might as well go in there and tell him I blew
11   up the Hindenburg and sunk the Titanic. *(#2 doesn't say*
12   *anything.)* What, no witty retort? — or maybe you've seen the
13   light. *(#2 is smiling.)*
14 #2: Actually, I was just thinking of that little business trip I took to
15   Japan last month.
16 #1: What the hell does that have to do with anything?
17 #2: Well, I'm not sure if you've ever been there, but they have some
18   of the most amazing stuff. Like this — *(#2 pulls a small device*
19   *out of his pocket.)*
20 #1: What is that?
21 #2: It's a very small, very efficient mini-recorder. Someone who
22   shall remain nameless and ever in my gratitude suggested to
23   me that something might be up with you. So this ... *(#2 holds*
24   *up the recorder)* was *my* little bit of preventative medicine in
25   case it was true. And look — it just happens to be on. I guess
26   I must have turned it on while you let me wait for twenty
27   minutes before you called me in here. And know what? — I
28   forgot to turn it off. Wow — what a lucky break for me. *(#2*
29   *stares at #1.)* What — no witty retort?
30 #1: You think my father will actually *buy* that?
31 #2: Yeah, I do. And what's more, you think so too. I'm sure he'll
32   love that part where you said — oh, what was that? — oh
33   yeah, "he's not particularly bright." How much you want to
34   bet that once he hears that he gets a real good case of the
35   smarts? *(#1 just stares.)*

1   **#1:** What do you want?

2   **#2:** Well, obviously, all my projects are still mine. See, believe it or

3   not — and you aside — I really like this company. I've got a

4   future here. Plus — and I'm sure you know about it — I

5   heard that in a couple of months another V.P. spot will

6   probably be opening up. And I plan to get it.

7   **#1:** And what makes you so sure you'll get it?

8   **#2:** 'Cause unlike you, I've worked really hard and I deserve it.

9   Besides, you'll have nothing to say about it, will you? *(#2*

10   *waves the recorder in front of #1. He/She doesn't say anything.)*

11   Didn't think so. And trust me, I will know if you try. Well, I

12   think that about covers everything. Have a nice day,

13   Jack/Jane. *(#2 starts to exit.)*

14 **#1:** You know, someday this company *will* be mine.

15 **#2:** Maybe, maybe not. But if it ever gets to that, I guess it'll be time

16   to move on. 'Cause knowing the way you work, if that

17   happens, this company will go under in a year — tops! But till

18   then ... *(#2 smiles, waves and exits. #1 slams his/her fist on the*

19   *desk and sits back.)*

20   **The End**

21

22

23

24

25

26

27

28

29

30

31

32

33

34

35

32. The Old Friend

CAST: #1, #2

SCENE OPENS: We are in a bar. #1 is sitting at the bar, having a drink and reading the paper. #2 enters, crosses to the bar, sits, and talks to the bartender.

#2: Sam, it's been a long week, and I could use a big drink. Let me have a gin and tonic. *(#2 puts down his/her paper and looks at #1.)*

#1: I thought you were a scotch drinker. *(#2 look at #1.)*

#2: Jeff/Judy?! Is that you?

#1: I haven't been gone that long, have I?

#2: No, I just didn't expect to see you here.

#1: I always liked this place. I try and wander in whenever I'm in town.

#2: So, what are you drinking?

#1: Beer. *(#1 turns towards the bartender.)*

#2: Well, Sam, you heard the man/woman. Let's get him/her another beer — on me.

#1: Thank you.

#2: How long *has* it been since you abandoned our happy little company to go into the evil world of politics?

#1: Two and a half years and I didn't go into politics.

#2: Wait, I thought ...

#1: I work for a political party.

#2: At the national level, right?

#1: Right.

#2: But you're not *in* politics?

#1: No. I like to think of myself as working — around politics.

#2: I see. Good answer.

#1: Well, it's the politically correct thing to say. *(They both laugh a little. #1 gets his/her drink and #2's drink.)*

#2: Here you go. *(They clink glasses.)*

#1: So, how are things around the company?

#2: I made vice president.

1 #1: That's great. Congratulations.

2 #2: Thanks. You remember James Caldwell? He died last year.

3 #1: Oh, that's too bad. He was a nice man.

4 #2: Yeah, he was. Outside of that, things are pretty much the same.
5   So, what brings you back to town?

6 #1: The national committee sent me here to head up one of the
7   campaigns for next month's election.

8 #2: Who are you campaigning for?

9 #1: Not who, what. I'm heading up the push for Proposition two-
10   fifteen. *(#2 stops and stares.)*

11 #2: Prop two-fifteen? You're opposing it, right?

12 #1: Hardly. It's one of the big propositions the party wants to see
13   passed. Why? Are you against it?

14 #2: Isn't anyone with a conscience? How can you back that? In all
15   the time we worked together, I never pegged you as a bigot.

16 #1: I'm not a bigot, and this proposition is not about bigotry.

17 #2: Really? Then what do you call cutting off basic human services
18   to non-English-speaking persons.

19 #1: That's not what two-fifteen does. It strengthens our national
20   borders and stops illegal immigrants from getting welfare,
21   and ...

22 #2: ... from getting medical care and food stamps. Basically it stops
23   them from getting a few of the necessities of life.

24 #1: It's amazing how you can make this so black and white. There's
25   a lot of gray area with this issue that you're not seeing.

26 #2: What gray area?! What are you saying, that these people by
27   consequence of their nation of birth should be left to fend for
28   themselves?

29 #1: No, but why should they get the same help as legal immigrants
30   and our own citizens and sometimes get it first?

31 #2: Because like it or not, these illegal immigrants are human
32   beings, and maybe, just maybe, some of them need the help ...
33   and yes, sometimes first.

34 #1: So, who's going to pay for all this? Where's all the money
35   supposed to come from?

1   #2: I don't know.

2   #1: Of course you don't. You just spout out some party line without

3   knowing all the intricate facts of the issue.

4   #2: I know what I'm talking about and there are a lot of people

5   who think exactly like I do.

6   #1: And even more who don't. Look, I've seen the data. Do you

7   know how many people are tired of going into a convenience

8   store and having to leave because no one speaks English? Do

9   you know that a lot of kids can't get minimum wage jobs

10   because employers give them to illegal immigrants whom they

11   can pay less? How about that our tax dollars go to people who

12   don't even pay taxes?

13   #2: And all problems will be solved by denying an infant a small

14   pox vaccine, right?

15   #1: *(Pause)* Are you truly this obtuse, or are just incredibly naive?

16   #2: OK, fine, you got me. I know it goes deeper than just a flu shot.

17   #1: Damn straight, it does. It's about our whole system.

18   #2: I'm almost afraid to ask this, but what do you mean "our whole

19   system"?

20   #1: Just that. The whole system stinks and Prop two-fifteen is the

21   first step in trying to right it.

22   #2: And after two-fifteen, what then? You planning on shutting

23   down the borders?

24   #1: Of course not, but I think it would behoove us to be a bit more

25   particular on who we let in. That's all I'm saying.

26   #2: And what, pray tell, do you and your little playmates plan to

27   use as your criteria? Credit rating, employment history …

28   *(Pause)* skin color?

29   #1: Why are you acting like this? I'm not your enemy. We've been

30   friends for years.

31   #2: No, we were friends for a short time years ago, but you're

32   right, you're not my enemy. The organization you work for,

33   however, is.

34   #1: You are taking this so personally. Why can't we just say that we

35   agree to disagree? That we have differing political ideologies,

1   leave it at that, and finish our drinks?
2 #2: Because you and your people scare me and because your
3   "ideologies" can't be ignored. Under the guise of "making a
4   better America" you're actually promoting bigotry and world
5   segregation. *(#2 gets up.)* So, you will excuse me if I don't just
6   "leave it at that." You'll also excuse me if I don't care to drink
7   with what I see as a fascist.
8 #1: You've got a lot of nerve. You can't call me that.
9 #2: *(#2 turns to the bartender.)* Let him pay for his own drink.
10 #1: You really haven't got a clue, do you?
11 #2: Sure I do. That's why I'm leaving. *(#2 exits.)*
12   The End
13
14
15
16
17
18
19
20
21
22
23
24
25
26
27
28
29
30
31
32
33
34
35

33. The Settlement

CAST: #1, #2

SCENE OPENS: We are in a conference room. #1, a lawyer, is going over a file. #2 knocks and enters.

#2: I'm sorry I'm late. I came over as soon as I got your message.

#1: It's OK. Sit down. *(#2 sits and looks at #1.)*

#2: So?

#1: So — I got a call from Dr. Winchell's attorney this morning. They want to settle. *(#2 pounds a fist on the table.)*

#2: I knew it! He was going to lose in court!

#1: Whoa, slow down.

#2: What's the matter? This is great. You don't seem very excited.

#1: Because it's not like they're just going to hand you some money and that's it. There are some conditions attached.

#2: I'm sure there are. First things first, how much money are we talking about?

#1: If we sign today ... one million.

#2: OK. That's what we figured we could get. I can live with that. Now — what about these conditions. *(#1 pulls a piece of paper out of the folder in front of him/her.)*

#1: You are not to discuss this case or anything about your mother's operation with anybody.

#2: *(Pause)* What else?

#1: Dr. Winchell will not admit to and not be held culpable in any way with regards to the death of your mother.

#2: Forget it!

#1: See, this is why I wasn't jumping up and down about this settlement. I knew this is how you would react.

#2: And you think my reaction is wrong?

#1: I didn't say that. I do, however think you should give it more than a nanosecond before coming to a decision.

#2: OK. *(Pause)* Forget it! That better?

#1: Fine. I'll reject the offer. We'll go to court if that's what you want.

1   #2: Wait a minute. I don't understand you. I thought you were on
2   my side. You said we could win this.
3   #1: We did! They're offering a million dollars. It's what we wanted.
4   #2: Correction, it's part of what we wanted. The other part was
5   getting Winchell to admit what he did.
6   #1: Don't you think that's what he's doing?
7   #2: No, I don't. He's paying me hush money. But I want other
8   people aside from you and me to know that ... that he killed
9   my mother. *(#1 looks at #2.)*
10   #1: I ... no, never mind.
11   #2: What? You were about to say something.
12   #1: Yeah, I was, but you weren't going to like it.
13   #2: I want to hear what you have to say.
14   #1: *(Pause)* OK, but you have to let me finish before you jump
15   down my throat.
16   #2: Sure.
17   #1: Andy/Andrea — I think you're wrong about Winchell.
18   #2: What?! How can ...
19   #1: You said you were going to let me finish. *(#2 stops.)* Now, I said
20   a lot of things about him to get him to pay, and we all know
21   that he's responsible, but the man's not a bad person. The
22   truth is — he made a mistake.
23   #2: Yeah, a mistake that killed my mother!
24   #1: Yes, you're right. His action, his mistake, led to the death of
25   your mother, but it wasn't intentional. It wasn't a deliberate
26   act.
27   #2: That doesn't make any difference.
28   #1: If you had been involved in as many of these cases as I have, you
29   might not say that.
30   #2: What does that mean?
31   #1: It means that I've seen some real butchers. Men and women
32   who should have never been given a medical license. People I
33   wouldn't let change the oil in my car but were still allowed to
34   cut others open. And unlike Winchell, they didn't care at all
35   about what they did.

1 #2: And Winchell cares so much he doesn't want anyone to find out
2   about this.
3 #1: If you were in his place — would you? I did some checking and
4   I found out that the accidental nicking of an artery is not all
5   that rare. Usually they're caught before closing. Unfortunately,
6   in this case it wasn't. Then there was your mother's age —
7   which made the operation more risky and her susceptibility to
8   shock greater.
9 #2: So what exactly are you trying to tell me here?
10 #1: I'm trying to help you see the whole picture before you make
11   your decision. Let me ask you something — why did you go to
12   Winchell in the first place?
13 #2: He was highly recommended. I was told he ... was the best.
14 #1: I assumed you checked him out. Did he ever have any suits
15   brought against him before?
16 #2: *(Pause)* No.
17 #1: As a matter of fact — his record was spotless. He's one of the
18   most well-respected doctors in the country in his field.
19 #2: And that means I'm supposed to forgive him?
20 #1: No, it means you should try and look past your anger.
21 #2: You still haven't given me a good reason why I should.
22 #1: *(Pause)* Ever made a mistake on the job, Andy/Andrea?
23 #2: Of course.
24 #1: Did any of these mistakes ever effect anyone else?
25 #2: Once, there were some regrettable repercussions for someone
26   else.
27 #1: Did what you did ever happen before? Did you make amends?
28 #2: No, it had never happened before or since and yes, I made
29   amends. And before you continue, I know where you're going
30   with this. When it was over, it was over, but ...
31 #1: No buts. Why should it be different for this man? Your
32   mistakes didn't come out in the papers. They didn't stop you
33   from continuing to do your job.
34 #2: But his mistake was bigger ...
35 #1: No, the repercussions were.

1   #2: Whatever — it doesn't really matter because the profession
2   he's chosen is much more lucrative and with that comes a
3   truly life and death risk factor, more responsibility, and more
4   accountability if a mistake is made.
5   #1: And he's being accountable. He's suspended from surgery for a
6   while, he's agreed to pay you and he's planning to do it out of
7   his own pocket. All he's really asking is that you allow him to
8   continue practicing medicine, because Winchell's saved a lot
9   of people …
10 #2: And killed one.
11 #1: Well, that's where we see how much compassion you have for
12   someone who made a mistake. *(#2 picks up the document.)*
13
14   **Ending 1**
15   *(#2 tears up the document.)*
16 #2: Absolutely none! The man killed my mother and I believe that
17   if he made that mistake — even once — he could make it
18   again. And if I can spare anyone else from going through what
19   I've been through — that's where I should focus my energies.
20   Not towards saving Winchell's career.
21 #1: I think you'll regret this in the long run. Who knows, we may
22   even lose in court.
23 #2: I'll take that chance. And if you don't agree — you can quit
24   right now and I'll get someone who's completely in my corner.
25 #1: I told you from the beginning that I was on your side and I'll
26   follow through with whatever you wish. I just felt it was my
27   duty to let my feelings on the matter be known.
28 #2: They're duly noted. *(Pause)* Reject the offer! *(#2 gets up and
29   leaves.)*
30
31   **Ending 2**
32   *(#2 signs the document.)*
33 #1: I think you're making the wise decision.
34 #2: Trust me, it's not really out of compassion for the man.
35 #1: Well, I hope it's not totally mercenary.

1	#2:	Why do you really care either way? You'll get your third. But
2		if you must know — I just realized how tired I am of the
3		whole thing. I don't want to argue anymore or debate the
4		issue. And if I take him to court, it'll just go on and on. So,
5		maybe his payment is somewhat of an admission; then again,
6		maybe not. But either way, it's probably the best I'll ever get
7		and it'll be over. *(Pause)* I will tell you something, though.
8	#1:	What?
9	#2:	If the man does make this kind of mistake again — it'll be on
10		your head, not mine.
11	#1:	Let's just pray that he doesn't.
12	#2:	You pray. I'm done. My conscience is clear. *(#2 gets up and*
13		*hands #1 the document.)* **Just get my check.** *(#2 exits.)*
14		**The End**
15		
16		
17		
18		
19		
20		
21		
22		
23		
24		
25		
26		
27		
28		
29		
30		
31		
32		
33		
34		
35		

34. The Session

CAST: DOCTOR, PATIENT

SCENE OPENS: The DOCTOR is seated in a chair in the office reading a file. The PATIENT enters. They stare at each other for a moment.

DOCTOR: Are you going to sit?

PATIENT: I don't know. I haven't decided whether I'm going to stay or not.

DOCTOR: When you make your decision, be sure to let me know. *(The DOCTOR goes back to reading a file. The PATIENT stares for a few moments more, then sits. The DOCTOR closes the file.)*

PATIENT: You're not going to take any crap from me, are you?

DOCTOR: I don't have to. It's not in my job description.

PATIENT: Touché.

DOCTOR: Let me make this as plain as I can for you. You are here for thirty days observation and we can play it anyway you want.

PATIENT: Well, that's the point then, isn't it?

DOCTOR: What?

PATIENT: I don't think I need to be "observed" by you or anyone else.

DOCTOR: You don't?

PATIENT: Didn't I just say that? What's the problem? Don't you understand English?

DOCTOR: Oh, I understand English just fine. *(Pause)* What makes you think you don't need to be here?

PATIENT: What makes you think I do? I'm fine.

DOCTOR: I see. So, your life is all lollipops and sunshine?

PATIENT: You bet!

DOCTOR: Then why did you attempt suicide?

PATIENT: *(Pause)* I was bored. There was nothing on cable that night.

DOCTOR: Let me rephrase the question. Why did you try to kill

1   yourself at your parent's house?

2   PATIENT: Because none of my friends would let me use their

3   houses.

4   DOCTOR: Are you planning on giving me a straight answer?

5   Because I can't help you if you don't.

6   PATIENT: I don't need your help.

7   DOCTOR: Your parents seem to think you do. That's why they put

8   you in here.

9   PATIENT: Well, that's their problem and their opinion.

10   DOCTOR: And what's your opinion?

11   PATIENT: I told you. I'm doing just fine.

12   DOCTOR: Does it make sense to you that someone who is "doing

13   fine" would try to commit suicide?

14   PATIENT: OK, you caught me. I know I've got some problems, but

15   I can handle them on my own. I prefer to handle them on my

16   own.

17   DOCTOR: Trying to kill yourself isn't handling. It's giving up.

18   PATIENT: Thanks for clarifying that for me.

19   DOCTOR: And what's wrong with asking for help?

20   PATIENT: Because you can't understand what I'm going through.

21   DOCTOR: Not if you don't explain it to me, I can't. I'm not here

22   to pass judgment on you. All I want to do is see if we can come

23   up with some answers, together.

24   PATIENT: Oh, please! Everyone passes judgment. That's the

25   nature of people and I'm fed up with it.

26   DOCTOR: Well, that's the first pertinent thing you've said. Why

27   do you think you're being judged?

28   PATIENT: Fine, I'll play your little shrink game. Why do you think

29   I think I'm being judged?

30   DOCTOR: I don't know. Why don't you just cut out the crap and

31   answer the question? Why do you think you're being judged?

32   PATIENT: Get lost!

33   DOCTOR: Wrong answer. *Why?!*

34   PATIENT: *Because I am! OK?!*

35   DOCTOR: *(Pause)* See, not so difficult. Now, who's judging you?

1   PATIENT: A better question would be, "Who isn't?"

2   DOCTOR: What about your parents?

3   PATIENT: Please. "You're not living up to your potential. You're

4   not dating the right person ... The Johnsons' son is a vice

5   president now ... Why don't you have a better apartment?

6   What would you call that?

7   DOCTOR: You're right, it's judgmental. Who else?

8   PATIENT: How about my ex-boss who said I wasn't producing as

9   much as everyone else. So I was fired. Then there's my fiancée

10   who thought we were in love, then just decided we weren't.

11   DOCTOR: Anyone else?

12   PATIENT: Isn't that enough for you?

13   DOCTOR: So, what I'm hearing is that you lost your job and your

14   fiancée, your parents are on your back and you decided to kill

15   yourself over it.

16   PATIENT: Well, thank you for minimizing my whole existence.

17   DOCTOR: I'm not minimizing anything. I'm just restating what

18   you've told me. Is what I said true?

19   PATIENT: Yes, it is, but it's much more than that.

20   DOCTOR: Tell me how.

21   PATIENT: I can't look at a newspaper or turn on the television

22   without being reminded that I don't have the right job,

23   car, ... clothes. That I don't have enough money or ... look

24   like I should be on the cover of a magazine ...

25   DOCTOR: Sounds to me like you're the one who's judging you.

26   PATIENT: Typical shrink answer. It's all my own fault.

27   DOCTOR: I didn't say that. Yes, you have pressure on you. Losing

28   your job and fiancée on top of each other is very traumatic —

29   but they didn't pry your mouth open and pour twenty plus

30   Seconal down your throat.

31   PATIENT: Convenient explanation.

32   DOCTOR: Maybe, but not as convenient as yours.

33   PATIENT: What does *that* mean?!

34   DOCTOR: You have a confidence problem. A pretty severe one, and

35   instead of recognizing it, you chose to blame the world for it.

1   PATIENT: I'm not blaming the world.

2   DOCTOR: OK, then if not the world, you're blaming the car

3   dealers, credit card companies, clothing manufacturers and

4   anyone else who might be advertising.

5   PATIENT: You're twisting what I said.

6   DOCTOR: Am I? You're not perfect and you're pissed off about it.

7   PATIENT: Who said I wanted to be perfect?

8   DOCTOR: What do you want, then?

9   PATIENT: I don't know!

10   DOCTOR: Oh, I think you do.

11   PATIENT: Who cares *what* you think?!

12   DOCTOR: Why don't you just answer the question? *What do you*

13   *want?!*

14   PATIENT: *More than I've got!* (Silence.)

15   DOCTOR: Tell me about the pills.

16   PATIENT: I really don't know. The whole thing seems so surreal now.

17   DOCTOR: Do your best.

18   PATIENT: You know how people talk about waking up in the

19   morning and not having a reason to get out of bed.

20   DOCTOR: Yes.

21   PATIENT: Well, for the longest time I didn't see any reason to get

22   up, go to bed ... or even wake up. It just seems ...

23   DOCTOR: Just seems what?

24   PATIENT: That I can't catch a break with anything. I look around

25   and see people with jobs they like ... and relationships that

26   are working. I see people who are ... happy with themselves

27   or just ... generally happy. Why can't I even have part of

28   that? Why can't any part of my life, for once, just work?

29   DOCTOR: Because you're not letting it. You are so busy comparing

30   what you do and who you're with and *who you are* — with

31   everything around you — that you can't possibly succeed. It's

32   not life not giving you a break. It's *you* not giving you a break.

33   PATIENT: So what do you suggest?

34   DOCTOR: Not a quick fix. That's for damn sure. I would suggest

35   we focus on *one* thing for right now. You pick it. If that takes

1   the whole thirty days ... so be it. If not, we'll go on from there.

2 PATIENT: *(Pause. Almost in tears)* I'm afraid.

3 DOCTOR: I know. You should be. You did something very drastic

4   and we're going to make damn sure it never happens again.

5   Do you believe me?

6 PATIENT: I'd like to.

7 DOCTOR: For the time being ... that's great. I'll see you

8   tomorrow. *(The PATIENT gets up and exits.)*

9   **The End**

10

11

12

13

14

15

16

17

18

19

20

21

22

23

24

25

26

27

28

29

30

31

32

33

34

35

35. The Strangers

CAST: MAN, WOMAN

SCENE OPENS: We are in a theatre. A young WOMAN in her early twenties, an actress, has just gotten off work. She is walking around the stage, stops and stares out at the audience. A MAN walks up behind her.

MAN: Hi. *(The WOMAN jumps.)*

WOMAN: God! You scared me.

MAN: I'm sorry. I didn't mean to.

WOMAN: Who are you and what are you doing here?

MAN: Nobody and just looking.

WOMAN: Only cast and crew are supposed to be in the theatre after the show.

MAN: I know, but I did a show here once and I'd thought I'd come here and look around.

WOMAN: Yeah. You look familiar. Do I know you?

MAN: I don't think so. I've just got one of those faces. What are you doing here?

WOMAN: Just thinking. Sometimes when the show's over I like to come out on stage by myself.

MAN: I know how you feel. It gets real quiet. It's kinda nice.

WOMAN: It is. Why didn't you ever work here again?

MAN: I tried, but I just haven't got another part in one of their shows. You know how it is.

WOMAN: Yeah, I do. So, what brings you here now?

MAN: Reminiscing. I met someone here.

WOMAN: A girl?

MAN: No, a goat. We got very close. Yes, a girl.

WOMAN: I met someone here too. What happened to yours?

MAN: She broke up with me. And you?

WOMAN: I broke up with him.

MAN: Why?

WOMAN: He got more serious than I wanted to. You?

1   MAN: I got more serious than she wanted.

2   WOMAN: Did you love her? *(He pauses.)*

3   MAN: Yeah, I did.

4   WOMAN: Did she love you? *(He pauses and thinks.)*

5   MAN: At times.

6   WOMAN: How do you love somebody "at times"?

7   MAN: Well, there were moments when she said she did and I knew

8   it was true. Then a lot of the time the feeling really scared her.

9   WOMAN: Why do you think that was?

10   MAN: She was a lot younger than I was. She confused love and age.

11   She told a mutual friend of ours that she didn't know what

12   love was. The thing is, I really didn't know myself. I may have

13   been older, but only felt that one other time in my life. Besides,

14   I think she wanted to be a kid a while more. You know, foot

15   loose and fancy free. That sort of thing. What about you?

16   WOMAN: Sounds a lot like my situation. I just didn't want to be

17   committed at the time.

18   MAN: Did you at least have a good time while you were going out?

19   *(She pauses and thinks. A smile comes over her face.)*

20   WOMAN: Yeah, we did. Did you stay in touch with your ex?

21   MAN: I tried, but she never responded. You know, that

22   disappointed me the most. She was pretty honest with me

23   except about that. She said she wanted to stay friends, but she

24   never followed through. I think she wanted to make things

25   easy on herself, so she cut me off. What about you? Did you

26   stay in touch?

27   WOMAN: Not really.

28   MAN: Do you ever miss him?

29   WOMAN: Yeah, I do. He was never anything but wonderful to me.

30   I wish it could have been different.

31   MAN: You know what really makes a relationship special?

32   WOMAN: What?

33   MAN: When you get something that no one has ever given you

34   before.

35   WOMAN: Like what?

1   MAN: Nothing material, something just ...

2   WOMAN: I think I know what you mean. My ex gave me something.

3   MAN: What?

4   WOMAN: A birth-weekend.

5   MAN: A what?

6   WOMAN: Birth-weekend. See, I used to spend part of the weekend
7   with him and my birthday was on a Sunday, but I couldn't be
8   with him, so he celebrated it on Thursday, Friday and Saturday.

9   MAN: I see, so you had a ...

10 BOTH: Birth-weekend.

11 WOMAN: Yeah. No one ever gave me that before.

12 MAN: What did he give you?

13 WOMAN: I don't really remember, but it's not important. It was
14   my special weekend. What about you?

15 MAN: You'll think I'm being corny.

16 WOMAN: No, I won't.

17 MAN: OK, see, she had these light blue eyes and when she would
18   look at me and smile it would go right through me. I guess you
19   could say she had a smile that touched my heart. I never had
20   that before.

21 WOMAN: I don't think that's corny. It's ... nice. God, we sound so
22   *damned* depressing.

23 MAN: Not just depressing, but *damned* depressing, huh?

24 WOMAN: Why did you say that?

25 MAN: No reason. Why?

26 WOMAN: Nothing, it just reminded me of ... someone. Anyway,
27   it's getting late. I gotta go.

28 MAN: Yeah. Me too. I don't work here anymore. They won't like
29   me hanging around. *(They start to exit in different directions.)*
30   Hey, thanks for listening.

31 WOMAN: You too. By the way, my name's Carrie.

32 MAN: Mine's Garry. *(They walk over and shake hands.)* Nice to meet
33   you. 'Bye.

34 WOMAN: 'Bye. *(They exit.)*

35   **The End**

36. The Testimony

CAST: #1, #2

SCENE OPENS: We are in an office/conference room. #1 is on the phone.

#1: I told you not to worry about it. They're calling their last witnesses today and only one is ours. *(Pause)* Yeah, I'm meeting with him/her in ... *(Checks watch/clock)* about thirty seconds. *(Pause)* I'll see you there. *(#1 hangs up the phone and presses an intercom.)* Janie, is Eddie/Emily out there? *(Pause)* Well, send him/her in. *(#2 enters.)*

#2: Hey, Jack/Janet. What's up?

#1: We need to talk.

#2: Can it wait? If I'm going to get to the deposition on time, I need to leave. Traffic's terrible going downtown this time of day.

#1: You'll get there in plenty of time. Sit down. Your deposition is what we need to talk about. *(#2 sits.)*

#2: I've got to testify. I was subpoenaed.

#1: I know, don't worry about it. I just want to talk to you about your testimony.

#2: What's to talk about? I'll answer the questions they ask me. Seems like a pretty simple concept.

#1: Maybe not as simple as you think. I just want to make sure that the answers you give ... are the correct ones.

#2: You mean that the answers I give are the honest ones, don't you?

#1: Honest, correct, what's the difference really? It's all in how you look at it. *(#2 looks at #1.)*

#2: Oh, I don't like the sound of this at all.

#1: Relax, we just want to know that what you say won't hurt the company.

#2: "*We* just want to know?" Did some other people come in that I didn't notice?

#1: I meant ... *I* want to know.

1   #2: No, you didn't. *(Pause)* **Mr. McSherry** sent you to talk to me,
2   didn't he?

3   #1: *(Pause)* **OK, yeah, he did, but he just wants to make sure that**
4   **you get the facts straight before you get deposed.**

5   #2: **All I know is that Jake Martin was working here one day, doing**
6   **a great job, then he wasn't working here the next day. Fired**
7   **for what seems like bogus reasons.**

8   #1: **See, this is all Mr. McSherry wants you to see. The reason**
9   **wasn't bogus. He had good reason for letting Jake go.**

10 #2: **Really? From what Jake told me, he was fired for not**
11   **producing enough profit from his client list and generally not**
12   **living up to his full potential.**

13 #1: **That's exactly right.**

14 #2: **Then how do you explain that the month before he was fired,**
15   **his clients accounted for almost half the firm's income that**
16   **month?**

17 #1: **That's simply not true.**

18 #2: **Yes, it is. And that client, Ambrose Toys, that quit and went to**
19   **another firm wasn't even Jake's. He was asked to take it over**
20   **when Susan quit, but Ambrose wanted Susan and followed**
21   **her to her new agency.**

22 #1: **See, you've got it all wrong and you're going to make a fool of**
23   **yourself if you say that.**

24 #2: **You know, this is the second time you've told me I was wrong.**
25   **I was there. Jack/Janet, I know what I know. Jake was a good**
26   **employee.**

27 #1: **Then why was he fired, huh? It's not good business practice to**
28   **fire top-notch people, now is it?**

29 #2: **No, it's not.**

30 #1: **No, especially if he's bringing in as much money as you say. So**
31   **what's the reason?** *(#2 rises.)*

32 #2: **I don't have to answer to you! I have to go.** *(#2 starts to exit.)*

33 #1: **That's right, you do. Just remember, if you don't get your facts**
34   **straight before you get there — you may not have a job to**
35   **come back to tomorrow.** *(#2 stops and turns back to #1.)*

1   #2: Are you threatening me?

2   #1: Just warning. Mr. McSherry would be very unhappy if

3   someone told lies about him.

4   #2: I see. *(Pause)* Thank you for telling me that. As long as you put

5   it that way I guess I should forgo testifying to what a good

6   employee Jake was ...

7   #1: That would be for the best.

8   #2: And jump straight to what I really know, and that is that

9   McSherry fired Jake because he was gay! Period, end of story.

10   You know it and I know it!

11   #1: I know nothing of the kind! That is a bold-faced lie!

12   #2: Knock it off, Jack/Janet! Why don't you just cut out all this

13   crap and be straight with me? You can show me as much

14   trumped-up evidence as you want on how Jake was a bad

15   employee, but as far as my testimony goes, there's one thing

16   you can't fight.

17   #1: And what's that?

18   #2: I have nothing to gain if Jake wins this suit. So ... why would I

19   lie?

20   #1: Maybe because Jake is a friend of yours.

21   #2: And so are you. As a matter of fact, until all this started, Jake

22   was a good friend of yours too. But all of that aside, you still

23   haven't answered my question; why would I lie about it? *(#1*

24   *is silent for a moment.)*

25   #1: OK, let's suppose for a moment, and this is strictly

26   hypothetical, that you're right. Doesn't McSherry have the

27   right to employ or not to employ anyone he wants?

28   #2: No — McSherry doesn't have that right. If he had actually

29   interviewed Jake, he wouldn't have had to hire him. But

30   considering Jake was already here when McSherry took over

31   from his father, what he did was illegal.

32   #1: But it can't be proved!

33   #2: Oh, no? Before McSherry was boss we all hung out sometimes.

34   I don't think there's one person who hadn't heard his

35   homophobic speech when he'd had a couple of drinks. Then

1   when he became president, Jake got worried. And obviously
2   he had good reason. Bottom line — he's a bigot.
3   #1: If that's how you feel, why are you still here? How can you, in
4   all good conscience, work for a man like that?
5   #2: Because I have a feeling he won't be here that long. The press
6   may not know about all this yet, but they will if this goes to
7   trial. That aside, our board of directors does know and for a
8   company that's just beginning to be a major player, this is a
9   highly undesirable but correctable situation. But what I'd
10   really like to know is why you're being this guy's triggerman?
11   #1: Look, Eddie/Emily, when I got promoted ... it's just that ...
12   I've got a family, a house and bills. I simply can't afford a
13   conscience.
14   #2: That's sad, Jack/Janet, that's really sad. But be careful, 'cause
15   when this guy goes down, I don't think he'll be alone.
16   #1: Then you'd better watch it too. A lot can happen before then.
17   Can't it?
18   #2: We'll have to see. *(#2 starts to exit.)*
19   #1: Eddie/Emily — when it's over, I hope we — you and I — can
20   get past all this.
21   #2: See, Jack/Janet, that's the difference between us — I don't
22   want to get over it. *(#2 exits.)*
23   **The End**
24
25
26
27
28
29
30
31
32
33
34
35

37. The Caseworker

CAST: #1, #2

SCENE OPENS: We are in a basement corridor of a hospital, outside the morgue. #1, a social worker, is waiting. #2 enters and goes up to #1.

#1: Where have you been? I paged you over an hour ago.

#2: I was trying to be incommunicado. This was supposed to be my first night off in a month.

#1: Yeah, well, me too.

#2: Then what are we doing here?

#1: Well, I was about to leave the office and they asked me to come over here and drop off some paper work for two of my geriatric cases. Then as I was about to leave, the office called trying to find you. You still haven't given the office your other pager number, have you?

#2: No. Social Services isn't paying me enough to be on call ninety hours a day, eight days a week. So, what's up? And I already hate the fact we're standing outside the morgue.

#1: Someone reported a dead woman to the police. No ID on her, but your card was in her pocket. Then the same someone told the police they thought it was Betty Johnson.

#2: Oh, no!

#1: They need a positive ID. Since your card was in the pocket …

#2: Yeah, yeah, I get it.

#1: You want me to go in with you?

#2: No. Wait here. *(#2 goes into the morgue. #1 starts looking at the file. After a beat, #2 comes back out.)* **Damn!**

#1: I take it that's a positive ID.

#2: She was pretty badly beaten, but it was her. Let me see that file. Do the police have any idea who it might be?

#1: They think it was Betty's stalker.

#2: That's impossible. That animal's locked up.

#1: No, he's not.

1   #2: Yes, he is. Six months ago. I was sitting in court with Betty
2   when the judge gave him a year. I was pissed because he
3   didn't get five.
4   #1: Yeah, well apparently they kicked him loose last week.
5   #2: What in God's name for?
6   #1: Overcrowding. They decided he'd served enough time and they
7   needed the space.
8   #2: I don't believe this system.
9   #1: I guess they figured he could help the overcrowding problem on
10   the outside by eliminating people one by one. *(#2 looks at #1.)*
11   #2: That's not funny.
12   #1: I guess not. I'm sorry.
13   #2: There's a really nice woman in that room who happens to be
14   dead and you're making jokes.
15   #1: I said I was sorry. You don't have to take my head off.
16   #2: *(Pause)* I'm not mad at you. I'm mad at myself.
17   #1: Why?
18   #2: Because I obviously couldn't help her.
19   #1: You did everything you could.
20   #2: If that were true, she wouldn't be lying on a slab in there. And
21   a little boy would still have his mother. *(#2 suddenly realizes*
22   *something.)* Oh no — Robert ...
23   #1: Relax, he's been taken care of. The cops took him over to
24   juvenile hall.
25   #2: Robert's never going to forgive me. I gave him my word his
26   mom would be OK.
27   #1: This isn't your fault!
28   #2: Really? Let's play a little role reversal. You're a nine-year-old
29   kid. Some guy is stalking your mom. A man/woman from the
30   government comes to your house and promises that the guy
31   won't hurt Mom anymore. Mom winds up dead. Who do you
32   blame? The stalker? No, he was always the bad guy. You
33   blame the man/woman from the government who lied and
34   said Mom would be OK.
35   #1: It's more complicated than that.

1   **#2:** Not to a nine-year-old it isn't. And the truth is, he'd be right. I
2   lied. I said Betty would be fine and she's dead. Period!
3   **#1:** Betty is dead because she had a stalker. You held this woman's
4   hand, took her to the hospital, got a restraining order, got the
5   courts to lock the stalker up, helped her get a job and find a
6   new place. What more are you supposed to do? Stand guard
7   twenty-four hours a day?
8   **#2:** And look at the final results of all that work. *(#2 pushes a*
9   *Polaroid picture in #1's face.)*
10 **#1:** Take that away!
11 **#2:** No — take a good look. That's Betty's face, or what's left of it.
12   Want a copy? There's a whole stack of these in there. *(#1*
13   *pushes the picture away.)*
14 **#1:** What do you want me to say?
15 **#2:** Just admit that we can't do anything and the system sucks.
16 **#1:** Saying the system sucks is redundant, but I believe that we do
17   the best we can, and we do help people.
18 **#2:** Really? If you listen carefully, you might hear Betty laughing in
19   there.
20 **#1:** You know what? If you want to be a martyr over this, then go
21   to the nearest cliff and throw yourself off. Otherwise, give it a
22   rest.
23 **#2:** Nice response from a social worker.
24 **#1:** Fine! Here's the truth. I believe that this guy would have killed
25   Betty no matter what we did, and if you were there, he
26   probably would have gone through you to get to her.
27 **#2:** And you think that's an answer?
28 **#1:** No, and it's not fair either, but then neither was my mother
29   dying of cancer at fifty. But that wasn't her doctor's fault.
30   Sometimes things happen despite your best efforts.
31 **#2:** So if you cut away all the crap and rhetoric, what your basically
32   saying is, you win some and lose some.
33 **#1:** *(Pause)* Yeah, I guess I am.
34 **#2:** Not much of a philosophy of life.
35 **#1:** Wasn't meant to be. Just a statement of fact.

1 #2: Well, I don't know if I can be in a business anymore where we
2   seem to lose more than we win.
3 #1: Do you know how many times you've said that?
4 #2: I mean it this time. *(Pause)* No, I don't. I'll be right back at the
5   office Monday — complaining — won't I?
6 #1: I'd bet on it. Of course, you'll be late. You're always late on
7   Mondays. *(#2 is thinking.)*
8 #2: Hey, who's that guy we know at the *Times*? The one who works
9   Metro. Dan … ?
10 #1: Dan Kushner?
11 #2: Yeah, Dan Kushner.
12 #1: What about him?
13 #2: You think he'd find Betty's story and picture interesting? Do
14   you think he'd find a story in how the system screwed up?
15 #1: Probably. Do you know that if you do that you'll be stepping on
16   a whole lot of toes and causing a whole lot of controversy?
17 #2: And I should care about that because …
18 #1: You shouldn't and you won't. Being you that's just par for the
19   course. Let's get out of here. I'll buy you a drink. *(They start*
20   *to exit. #2 looks back at the morgue door.)*
21 #2: You go ahead. I wanna say good-bye to Betty. Let her know I'm
22   sorry. Understand?
23 #1: Yeah. I do. See you Monday.
24 #2: Late as usual. *(#2 goes into the morgue. #1 watches, then exits.)*
25   **The End**
26
27
28
29
30
31
32
33
34
35

38. The Decision

CAST: #1, #2

SCENE OPENS: We are in a lawyer's office. #1, a lawyer, is at a desk
going over a file. #2 knocks.

#1: Come in. *(#2 enters.)* Can I help you?

#2: I'm looking for Martin/Mary Nelson. My name is Sam/Samantha
Carter.

#1: Phyllis Carter's son/daughter.

#2: Yes.

#1: Please, come in. Sit down. *(#2 sits.)* I am so sorry about your
mother.

#2: Thank you.

#1: You live in California, don't you? When did you get in?

#2: This morning. I went to the hospital, saw my mother and talked
with my father and sister. They gave me your name and I
came right here.

#1: So what can I do for you?

#2: For starters you can tell me what's going on.

#1: How much do you know?

#2: From what the doctors tell me, my mother had a major stroke
with irreversible vascular damage. For all intents and
purposes, she's dead. No brain activity. But she's being kept
alive by machines that my father wants to turn off, but the
group called "Life's Coalition," for which you are the legal
representative, has blocked the hospital from turning
anything off. Am I correct so far?

#1: Well, you have the basic facts. I'm not just the legal
representative. I'm a member of the group. One of our members
met your mother in church, and Phyllis joined this organization
about a year ago. She was at one of our rallies when she had her
stroke. We've been at her side the whole time.

#2: I know. I saw someone at the hospital. And really, I appreciate
the help and comfort you're trying to give, but according to

1   her doctors, my mother has no chance for recovery. So ...

2   what do you think you're doing to her?

3   #1: We're not "doing" anything. We are just looking after her best

4   interests.

5   #2: "Her best interests"? I know for a fact that this is not what she

6   would want.

7   #1: And just how do you know that?

8   #2: Because she told me. When her mother died, she lingered for a

9   very long time. My mother said that she would never want

10   that to happen to her. She said she would just want to get it

11   over with and not just be kept alive.

12 #1: When was this?

13 #2: Uh ... ten years ago.

14 #1: And when's the last time you actually *saw* your mother?

15 #2: About a year ago, why?

16 #1: Because you would have no real way of knowing how she felt

17   now, would you? The facts are, she's changed quite a bit since

18   her mother died and a lot in the last year.

19 #2: OK, I haven't *seen* her in a year, but I wasn't out of touch. I've

20   talked with her a lot. She hadn't changed that much.

21 #1: And you're so sure about that? Did your mother tell you in the

22   last year that she would want her life support turned off if she

23   were in this ... situation?

24 #2: No, but —

25 #1: Then we really have nothing to discuss, do we? *(#1 starts to go*

26   *back to some papers.)*

27 #2: Wait a minute, I'm being dismissed? Who the hell do you think

28   you are?

29 #1: I will thank you to watch your language in this office!

30 #2: Watch my language? My mother is clinically dead, you won't

31   let her die in peace, and you're going to admonish me for my

32   language? Why don't you go —

33 #1: *(Cutting #1 off)* Look, I'm warning you ...

34 #2: No! You don't warn me about a thing! I warn you! Who are you

35   to dictate what we can do about my mother?!

1   #1: I am simply carrying out her will.

2   #2: Really?! Then you'd better produce her conscious and

3   articulate so I can hear it for myself! And if you can't do that,

4   maybe you have a memo ... or ... a fax that proves that she's

5   empowering you to act for her. My mother is already dead.

6   #1: Not in our eyes. As long as there is breath in her body ...

7   #2: But the breath isn't there, it's being created.

8   #1: She's alive! It's our intention to keep her that way.

9   #2: And who's supposed to pick up the tab?

10   #1: Our organization may be able to help find some financial —

11   #2: I wasn't talking about money. I mean, who's going to deal with

12   the emotional costs to my father, my sister ... me?

13   #1: *We* are always here to comfort.

14   #2: You? You're going to comfort us? That's very big of you

15   considering you're the ones who are prolonging the pain and

16   putting us in this position in the first place.

17   #1: You have no idea who we are and what our organization is all

18   about. There are millions of people who believe in us, who are

19   a part of our family and find a lot of comfort and tranquility

20   with us.

21   #2: You're absolutely right. I don't know anything about you, but I

22   do know that my father thinks your organization is crap and

23   wasn't happy that my mother was a part of it. And that, my

24   friend, is a fact.

25   #1: Your father doesn't believe in us, well, that's his right. But your

26   mother is a member and it's she that we're concerned about.

27   #2: And my father has been told by his doctors that she, his wife of

28   forty-plus years, is gone and he believes them. That is also his

29   right, but he's not being allowed to accept that and deal with

30   his grief because you're keeping her artificially alive, saying

31   that she may come back to him.

32   #1: Can you tell me, absolutely, that it won't happen?

33   #2: Can you tell me that it will?

34   #1: I don't have to. That's called "faith." *(We are at a standoff.)*

35   #2: You know, I was brought up to believe that faith and ... belief

1   were good things. And I still do, but when one's beliefs

2   impinge upon another's, they're not good anymore. They're

3   selfish and in this case potentially destructive.

4   #1: To whom?

5   #2: My father. And trust me, you're going to need a lot more than

6   faith to protect yourself from me if my father has to go

7   through anymore unneeded misery.

8   #1: Please, don't even attempt to threaten me. I handle people like

9   you all the time. *(Pause)* I have them for lunch. You're not

10   scaring me, and if you try and come up against me, your

11   suffering will be a lot more than emotional ... I'll break you.

12   #2: *(Pause)* Careful counselor, your true colors are coming out.

13   *(Pause)* I'm leaving. *(#2 starts to exit.)* But here's a piece of

14   advice — I don't intimidate and I'll go to any lengths to

15   protect my family. You can take *that* on faith! *(#2 exits.)*

16   **The End**

17

18

19

20

21

22

23

24

25

26

27

28

29

30

31

32

33

34

35

39. The Tenant

CAST: #1, #2

SCENE OPENS: We are in an apartment. #1 is sitting on the couch doing some work. There is a knock on the door. #1 answers it. #2 is there.

#1: Oh, hi. How are you doing?

#2: Fine. Can I come in for a minute?

#1: Sure, I'm sorry. Come on in. *(#2 enters.)* Can I get you anything?

#2: I could use a glass of water.

#1: Coming right up. *(#1 exits to get the water.)* Make yourself at home. *(#2 looks around, then sits. #1 reenters with a glass of water and hands it to #2.)*

#2: Thanks. *(#1 sits.)*

#1: So, what can I do for you?

#2: We missed you at the co-op meeting last night.

#1: I know. I'm sorry, but things ran late at work and I didn't get home until after the meeting was over.

#2: Well, that's why I'm here. I want to fill you in on what was discussed.

#1: Great. Are we finally going to get the lobby repainted and carpeted?

#2: We really didn't discuss that at this meeting. We had a more serious … situation that developed.

#1: Really? What's that?

#2: I'm afraid we have an undesirable tenant living here.

#1: Really? I haven't heard anything about anyone being trouble.

#2: We just found out about him. We decided to get a petition together and present it to the building's board and ask to have him removed.

#1: This does sound serious. Who is it?

#2: Do you know Robert Sherman? He lives in Twelve-G.

#1: Yeah, I do. Always seemed like a nice guy.

1   #2: Well, he has a problem and we want him to leave before it
2   becomes our problem.
3   #1: What's the problem?
4   #2: He has ... AIDS.
5   #1: *(Pause)* That poor guy.
6   #2: I know. We all feel sorry for him.
7   #1: But you still want him out. Why?
8   #2: None of us want ... that around here. Do you?
9   #1: Personally, it's not my business, and frankly, it's none of yours
10   either.
11 #2: When it affects others it's not only his business.
12 #1: How is it affecting you or anyone else in the building?
13 #2: For one, what do you think it's going to do to the value of our
14   homes if it gets out that there's an AIDS patient living here?
15 #1: I'm sorry — what do you think he's going to do, take an ad out
16   in the *Times*?
17 #2: No, I don't think he'll do that, but word does get out. But
18   what's more of an immediate concern is that he's putting all
19   of us at risk by being here.
20 #1: *(Pause)* How? *(#2 doesn't answer.)* What, no answer?
21 #2: Let's just say that nobody knows all the facts. Do you?
22 #1: Obviously I know a lot more than you. See — I read. You ought
23   to try it sometime.
24 #2: The bottom line is that some of us just aren't ... comfortable
25   with him living here anymore.
26 #1: Well it all might be moot since he's paid for his apartment and
27   I don't see that there's anything you can do.
28 #2: I wouldn't be so sure. When Mr. Sherman applied to live here
29   and had his interview, he never mentioned his condition ...
30 #1: Or his lifestyle? But then again he didn't have to, and it would
31   have been against the law for you to ask. Just for the record,
32   how did you find out?
33 #2: Mr. Johnson, who lives next door, heard him talking on the phone.
34 #1: So the only reason you know is because you invaded his privacy?
35 #2: He left his door open. He invited it.

1   **#1:** Oh, that'll stand up. You are really something. There's a poor
2   sick man who should be receiving our support and you want
3   to make him homeless too.
4   **#2:** Hey, I'm sorry that he's sick, but it is my right whether I want
5   to associate with him or … his … with him or not.
6   **#1:** And it's his right to live where he chooses. Since Robert moved
7   in, have you ever socialized with him? Let's make it easier, have
8   you ever said "hi" to him? *(There is a silence.)* No, of course you
9   haven't. I'm sure *you*, or any of your friends, wouldn't.
10 **#2:** And just what do *you* mean by that?
11 **#1:** Well, God forbid anybody be different from you. What you and
12   your buddies need to remember is that it's not nineteen-fifty
13   anymore. Bigotry is no longer acceptable. Whatever happened
14   to caring, to compassion? Would it make any difference if
15   Robert were dying of cancer?
16 **#2:** Of course it would! That's acceptable.
17 **#1:** Well, on his behalf let me apologize. What bad taste he has to
18   contract a disease that's not acceptable to you.
19 **#2:** I've heard enough. You talk about his rights. What about my
20   rights? And other people's rights? I'm not the only one who
21   feels this way.
22 **#1:** That doesn't make you right, just ignorant.
23 **#2:** Say what you want, it doesn't matter. In this country I still have
24   the right to say what I want, feel what I want, and the right to
25   live in an environment that I feel is morally correct. And if I
26   feel that something is wrong, I do have the right to do
27   something about it!
28 **#1:** Get out. *(#2 gets up and starts to exit. He/she stops at the door and*
29   *turns back.)*
30 **#2:** Let me remind you of one thing. We can get undesirables out of
31   this building and undesirable doesn't just mean his kind.
32 **#1:** Oh, please, tell me you just said what I think you said. Is that a
33   threat? *(Silence)* No — well, let me say this. You may forget
34   that I'm a lawyer and if you or any of your "friends" make
35   one move against Robert, I will represent him for free and sue

1   you so fast you won't know what hit you. And by the time I'm
2   done, Robert will not only still be here, he'll probably own this
3   building.
4   #2: Now who's threatening who?
5   #1: Not "who," "whom" — and I am. I'm just protecting *my* moral
6   environment.
7   #2: You haven't heard the last of this.
8   #1: Oh, I'm sure I have. *(#1 picks up #2's clipboard.)*
9   #1: Hey bigot, you forgot your clipboard. *(#1 tosses the clipboard on*
10 *the floor in front of #2. He/she picks it up, looks and exits.)*
11   **The End**
12
13
14
15
16
17
18
19
20
21
22
23
24
25
26
27
28
29
30
31
32
33
34
35

40. The Escort

CAST: #1, #2

SCENE OPENS: We are in an apartment. #1 is on the couch watching a newscast about a clinic shooting. There is a knock on the door. #1 answers it. #2 enters.

#1: What are you doing here? I was just watching the report on the news.

#2: I was coming back from the police station and I got your message. I thought I'd stop by and let you know that I was OK. *(#1 and #2 sit down.)*

#1: What the hell happened? The news report didn't say anything.

#2: Well, I was assigned to the Westside Clinic today. I was escorting Dr. Hope from her car when this nut jumps out of the bushes with a gun and starts shooting.

#1: How many shots did he fire?

#2: I'm not sure. The whole thing happened so fast. Nobody knew what was happening.

#1: Was anyone hurt?

#2: No ... amazingly. It's lucky the guy was a lousy shot.

#1: Did they get him?

#2: Nope. That's why I was at the police station. With my description, they're pretty sure they know who it was.

#1: I can't believe how calm you are.

#2: You should have seen me three hours ago. I'm gonna make a drink. *(#2 starts to make a drink.)*

#1: Well, at least it's over and you won't have to be put in that position anymore.

#2: What do you mean?

#1: You quit, didn't you? You're not going to be a clinic escort anymore. *(Pause)* Are you?

#2: Why wouldn't I be?

#1: Because you were shot at! You could have been killed.

#2: But I wasn't and my position hasn't changed.

1 #1: Pretty cavalier attitude. Most people wouldn't put —

2 #2: I'm not most people.

3 #1: Well, that's for damned sure because most people have more

4   brains than that.

5 #2: Than what?

6 #1: Than what? Than putting themselves in the position of being a

7   walking target! Putting themselves at risk.

8 #2: You get in a car every day, don't you? That's taking a big risk.

9 #1: You're not really going to try and compare the two, are you?

10 #2: Well, a risk's a risk.

11 #1: And stupid is stupid.

12 #2: Hey, don't hold back. Tell me what you're really thinking.

13 #1: I'm sorry. I just don't understand why you're doing this.

14 #2: Because it's something that I truly believe in.

15 #1: So you believe in losing your life?

16 #2: That's not what I said, and you know it. We've had this

17   discussion before and we don't see eye-to-eye on this issue.

18   Let's just leave it at that.

19 #1: But in light of what's happened, one might think you'd have a

20   change of heart.

21 #2: What "one" would think that? You?

22 #1: *Anyone* who had a modicum of sense.

23 #2: I see. First I'm "stupid" and now I have "no sense." You're a

24   terrific friend. Thanks for the pep talk.

25 #1: I am your friend and I don't want to see you get killed.

26 #2: OK, I know you are and you care about my well-being, but let's

27   cut through the smoke screen and lay it all out. You and I have

28   opposing points of view on this issue and you are trying to use

29   this incident to prove *your* point of view.

30 #1: I don't have to prove anything and a lot of other people think

31   just like I do.

32 #2: What, you think that's some late-breaking story?! Hello — I

33   know that! So what should I do? Cave in because your side

34   decides it's OK to use violence now to get your point across?

35 #1: Don't put me in the same group as that guy today, and let me

1		ask you something. What gives you all the right to do what you
2		do?
3	#2:	We have a constitution that says so! See, this is a free country
4		and believe it or not, people do have a right to make decisions
5		*about* themselves, *for* themselves whether *you* like it or not.
6	#1:	And along with those rights goes a sense of responsibility. We
7		are *supposed* to have a higher sense of what's right and wrong.
8		And what goes on in those clinics is wrong!
9	#2:	According to whose set of rules? Also, tell me this. Where does
10		it all stop? Once you stop people from making decisions about
11		their own bodies — what's next? How much of my life and
12		everyone else's do you all want to control?
13	#1:	Stop twisting this around. We're talking about one thing and
14		that's what goes on there is murder and you know that!
15	#2:	*Don't tell me what I know!* (*#2 stops. There is a silence.*) Look,
16		this is a just a repeat of that same old song we've sung before.
17		We are on opposite sides of a very hot issue and we've still
18		managed to stay friends for a long time. Let's not blow that. I
19		respect your right to have your opinion and I think you should
20		respect mine.
21	#1:	I do, and believe it or not, my concern is *your* well-being right
22		now. I've been to meetings. There are a lot of … these kinds of
23		people around who did what that guy did today.
24	#2:	I know that. And I appreciate and thank you for your concern …
25	#1:	But you're going to keep doing the escort bit, aren't you?
26	#2:	Well, I wouldn't call it "the escort bit," but yeah, I am.
27	#1:	Why? Is it really worth your life?
28	#2:	I think so. I won't be bullied by someone trying to make his
29		point with a semiautomatic rifle. All it did was reaffirm my
30		convictions.
31	#1:	Well, I guess I have to admire you for that.
32	#2:	Only for that?
33	#1:	I've known you too long to admire you for anything else. (*#2*
34		*laughs a little.*)
35	#2:	Good point. Thanks for the drink. I'll talk to you this weekend.

1   *(#2 starts to exit.)*
2   **#1:** **Hey.** *(#2 turns back.)*
3   **#2:** **What?**
4   **#1:** **Be careful.**
5   **#2:** **I will.** *(#2 exits.)*
6   **The End**
7
8
9
10
11
12
13
14
15
16
17
18
19
20
21
22
23
24
25
26
27
28
29
30
31
32
33
34
35

Section Three
Multi-Person

41. The Commercial

CAST: JERRY (director), HERMAN (ad man), HELEN (actress),
MAN (with clapboard), ELEANOR (product inventor)

SCENE OPENS: There is general milling around of people preparing
to shoot a commercial. All characters are present. There is general
noise.

JERRY: OK, can we hold it down? Good, dynamite. OK, babes,
it's good to see you all here. I'm Jerry Twizzle, the director,
but you all know that. Next to me is Herman Crinkle from B
and H Advertising. Why don't you say, "Hi," guy.

HERMAN: *(Almost inaudible)* Hi.

JERRY: Great, Herman, great. Well, people let's get ready. It's
almost magic time. *(They all start to disperse.)* Helen, baby, can I
see you for a second? *(HELEN, the actress, walks over to JERRY.)*

HELEN: What?

JERRY: So, what do you think? You and me together again. It
must be kismet. Remember the great time we had after that
last commercial?

HELEN: I told you I never wanted to see your lecherous face again.
You're a sleaze, Jerry.

JERRY: I know you don't mean that. If you did, why are you here
now?

HELEN: They're paying me money, Jerry. If you'll excuse me. *(She
starts to leave, but he grabs her arm.)*

JERRY: Come on, give me another chance. I grow on people.

HELEN: So does fungus. *(She leaves. The rest all set up.)*

JERRY: OK, let's get started. Herman, you stay with me. *(They set
up. HELEN and ELEANOR stand next to each other. A MAN with
a clapboard holds it in front of the camera.)*

MAN: "Hemorrhoid Relief," take one.

JERRY: Action!

ELEANOR: Hello, I'm Dr. Eleanor Plug. I'm not an actress, but a
doctor who has spent the better part of the last ten years

1   developing this ... *(She indicates the box that HELEN is holding)*
2   Hemorrhoid Relief ...
3   JERRY: Cut, cut! Plug, honey, that was great. Helen, babe, I need
4   you to hold that higher. *(She raises the box.)*
5   HELEN: Here?
6   JERRY: Still higher, babe. *(She raises it to the side of her head, next*
7   *to her ear.)*
8   HELEN: How's that?
9   JERRY: Great. *(HERMAN goes over to JERRY.)*
10   HERMAN: Excuse me, Mr. Twizzle. Why is she holding that by
11   her ear?
12   HELEN: Because that's where he thinks it goes.
13   JERRY: Hey — funny. No, Herman, sweetheart, you can't see it,
14   you don't buy it. Capisce?
15   HERMAN: Yes — thank you. That's all I wanted to know. *(He sits*
16   *back down.)*
17   JERRY: OK — let's take it from the top.
18   MAN: "Hemorrhoid Relief," take two.
19   JERRY: Action!
20   ELEANOR: Hello. I'm Dr. Eleanor Plug. I'm not an actress, but a
21   doctor who has spent the better part of the last ten years
22   developing this. The Hemorrhoid Relief Device. The
23   revolutionary device is the first of its kind to alleviate the pain,
24   burning, and itching ...
25   JERRY: Cut, cut! Wait a minute. What is this? Let me see that
26   copy. *(He reads the script.)* This is no good. Who wrote this?
27   ELEANOR: I did.
28   JERRY: Herman, did you see this?
29   HERMAN: Well, to tell you the truth —
30   JERRY: Yeah, I thought so. It's no good.
31   ELEANOR: Why?
32   JERRY: It's too technical. There are too many scientific words.
33   ELEANOR: Hemorrhoid is too scientific?
34   JERRY: Yeah, whatever happened to those cute TV words that
35   explain it?

1   ELEANOR: Mr. Twizzle, this problem is not cute. People must be
2   informed of how revolutionary this product is. The scientific
3   advancements are astronomical. They —
4   JERRY: Hey, Doc, no offense, but nobody cares. All people want is
5   to feel ... comfortable. They want to ride bikes and swim. Go
6   dancing. Right, Herman?
7   HERMAN: Well ...
8   JERRY: Right. They don't want to learn how the damn thing
9   works. *(Shuddering)* Nobody does.
10   HERMAN: Now, hold on, we at B and H Advertising have decided
11   on a new policy of informing the public —
12   JERRY: Cram it, Crinkle!
13   HERMAN: Of course, you're right. Forgive me for speaking.
14   *(JERRY writes something down on a piece of paper.)*
15   JERRY: Now, read this on camera. *(ELEANOR and HELEN read*
16   *the paper.)*
17   HELEN: You've got to be kidding?! I can't read this.
18   JERRY: Sure you can. You're a natural. The camera loves you, babe.
19   HELEN: *No* — Then let me rephrase, I won't read this.
20   JERRY: Yeah. I'm pretty sure you will.
21   HELEN: Why should I?
22   JERRY: Because they're paying you. Remember?
23   ELEANOR: Well, I won't do it.
24   JERRY: Actually — they're paying you too. So what say we cut all
25   the discussion and do it?! *(They take their places.)*
26   MAN: "Hemorrhoid Relief," take three.
27   JERRY: Action!
28   ELEANOR: Hi, folks. I'm Dr. Ellie. If you get that ... you know,
29   uncomfortable feeling, try this cute new product. Hemorrhoid
30   Relief. You'll feel so good, you'll never know you had a problem.
31   HELEN: And it really, really works. *(ELEANOR nods in agreement.)*
32   JERRY: Cut, print! Perfect. Jerry, old boy, you've done it again.
33   **The End**
34
35

42. Next

CAST: HARRISON, KIRBY, PATTI

SCENE OPENS: HARRISON ADAMS is sitting at his desk. He is a producer/director and is in the process of auditioning actors for his new film. He speaks into his intercom.

HARRISON: Miss Berg, will you please send in the next two actors, please? *(HARRISON starts to write. The two actors, KIRBY and PATTI, enter. HARRISON doesn't look up. The ACTORS take a seat.)* **I'm Harrison Adams, the producer and director of "Nymphs from Neptune." I'll be right with you.**

KIRBY: Hi, I'm Kirby Bryant.

PATTI: Hi, I'm Patti Adams. *(HARRISON looks up.)*

HARRISON: Patti?

PATTI: Hi, Dad.

KIRBY: Dad?!

PATTI: Yes, Kirby, this is my father. *(KIRBY gets a bit nervous. He stands and extends his hand.)*

KIRBY: Hi, nice to meet you.

HARRISON: Shut up and sit down.

KIRBY: I can see that this is going to be a comfortable interview.

HARRISON: Patti, what the hell are you doing here?

PATTI: What do you think? I'm auditioning for the part of Organa, the Nymph from Neptune.

HARRISON: Over my dead body you are.

PATTI: Why not?

HARRISON: Uh ... this isn't your type of film.

PATTI: What's that suppose to mean? What is it ... a porno?

HARRISON: Of course not. You know that I don't make those kinds of films.

PATTI: Then what's the problem?

HARRISON: Let's just say that you're not right for the part.

KIRBY: Now, hold on. I've read the entire script and Patti seems to have ... all the essentials for the role.

1 HARRISON: And how do you know what my daughter has what's
2   essential?
3 KIRBY: Oh ... I mean ... I'm making an educated guess.
4 HARRISON: If I were you I'd educate myself on another subject.
5   *Clear?!*
6 KIRBY: Like fine crystal.
7 HARRISON: *Good!*
8 PATTI: Daddy, what's really the problem?
9 HARRISON: Nothing. You're just not right. That's all.
10 PATTI: *(Realizing)* Oh, I see what it is. You're upset because
11   Organa has to do a nude scene in the film.
12 KIRBY: She sure does.
13 HARRISON: Shut up, Kirby! See, that's why it's not right for you.
14   I don't want perverts like this educated guesser here, staring
15   at my daughter's butt, ten feet high.
16 PATTI: Oh, come on. I'm an actress and it's part of the role.
17   Besides, it's done tastefully.
18 HARRISON: I don't care. My daughter is not going to be shown
19   nude in public.
20 PATTI: Why not? You used to show those nude pictures of me on
21   the bearskin rug to everyone.
22 KIRBY: Really? That's pretty sick.
23 HARRISON/PATTI: Shut up, Kirby!
24 PATTI: You know it's true.
25 HARRISON: When I took those pictures you were seven months
26   old. Hardly the same thing.
27 PATTI: It was worth a shot.
28 HARRISON: So you can forget it. You're not reading.
29 PATTI: You can't do that. I'm a good actress and Kirby and I have
30   been rehearsing very closely.
31 HARRISON: How closely?
32 PATTI: Get your mind out of the gutter. I'm an actress and I want
33   to read.
34 HARRISON: I don't care.
35 PATTI: I'll tell my agent.

1   HARRISON: Go ahead.

2   PATTI: I'll tell the union.

3   HARRISON: Fine with me.

4   PATTI: *(Pause)* I'll tell mother!

5   HARRISON: Read. *(PATTI and KIRBY get up and prepare to read.)*

6   PATTI: You ready?

7   KIRBY: Sure. *(They start the scene.)*

8   PATTI: "Well, earthman, did you enjoy what Organa is capable
9   of?"

10   KIRBY: "I'll tell you lady, I ain't never felt anything like that
11   before. You must be from outer space."

12   PATTI: "Well, why don't you show me what Brooklyn-type
13   earthmen can do?"

14   KIRBY: "It would be my pleasure. You know, you nymphs from
15   Neptune are all alike." *(They start to embrace.)*

16   HARRISON: That will be enough. Thank you.

17   PATTI: But we haven't finished yet.

18   HARRISON: As far as I'm concerned, you have. I do have one
19   question though.

20   PATTI: What? *(HARRISON walks from his desk, over to KIRBY and
21   grabs him by the lapels.)*

22   HARRISON: I want to now what kind of rehearsals you had with
23   this ... troll!

24   KIRBY: It was nothing, just a little improvisation.

25   HARRISON: You should quit while you're ahead.

26   KIRBY: Sir, would I be correct in assuming at this point that you
27   are not going to give me the role?

28   PATTI: Daddy, let him go. This is hardly the kind of behavior one
29   would expect from a professional of your stature. *(HARRISON
30   lets him go.)*

31   HARRISON: So, you want professional? You've got it. *(HARRISON
32   walks back to his desk and sits.)* I'd like to thank you both for
33   coming in. If we need to see you again, we'll be in touch.

34   PATTI: But ...

35   HARRISON: That will be all Miss Adams. Thank you. Good-bye.

1   **PATTI: You wait till Mom hears about this. Come on, Kirby, let's**
2   **go.**
3   **KIRBY: Right.** *(They start to leave.)* **Wait, I forgot something.**
4   *(KIRBY walks back to HARRISON and gives him a picture.)*
5   **Here, I forgot to give you this.** *(HARRISON takes the picture,*
6   *crumples it and tosses it in the garbage can. Kirby watches this.)*
7   **Yeah, pretty much what I figured. Nice to meet you. Patti,**
8   **wait up.** *(They both exit. HARRISON takes a breath and pushes*
9   *the intercom button.)*
10   **HARRISON: Next!**
11   **The End**
12
13
14
15
16
17
18
19
20
21
22
23
24
25
26
27
28
29
30
31
32
33
34
35

Section Four
Monologs

43. Mickey

Mickey Mouse never came to my eighth birthday party. That may not seem like much now, but then, it was devastating. I see that you don't understand. OK, let me explain things. When I was a little kid, Mickey was my hero. I had all the stuff: the ears, the T-shirts, the socks, the shoes, the sheets, the towels, the lunch box, the posters. My room was decorated in early mouse, and I used to call my sister Minnie and my brother Goofy. My mother made me stop that. And of course, every afternoon I used to watch reruns of the old Mickey Mouse Club. I think ... I was the only kid in my neighborhood who knew the rest of the song after: "Saddle your ponies, here we go. Down to the talent rodeo ... " So, when my parents told me I could have a party for my eighth birthday, you know who I invited first. I was so excited that I didn't let my mother address that invitation. I did it myself and sent it to Mickey Mouse in care of Disneyland. It never occurred to me that he wouldn't show. I mean, I just saw him on TV a couple of days earlier getting an award or something in Washington and I lived in Baltimore, so it wasn't that much farther. I even told him I'd send the bus fare. So everything was set. The day of the party I was so happy. I'd set a place for Mickey at the backyard table next to me and I told my brother, Goofy, that if Mickey wanted to stay overnight, he'd have to sleep in the living room with our dog, Pluto. Well, the party started and all the kids came. At four o'clock when the parents came to pick everyone up, it finally dawned on me that he wasn't coming. This was a hell of a revelation on your eighth birthday. I ran into my room and locked the door and cried. My parents tried to get me to open up, but I wouldn't. This made my father upset and I heard him saying to my mother: "I can't believe he's so upset. He had a great party and I got him an autographed picture and glove from Brooks Robinson, the greatest baseball player in history, and he's crying because some five-foot rodent in red shorts didn't come." Dad didn't understand. Yeah, Brooks was great, but Mickey could hit and catch as well as him and it was harder for Mickey. He

only had four fingers on each hand. My mother understood though.
She came in later with a present. I opened it and it was a stuffed
Mickey and a letter. It was from Mickey and he said he was sorry
he couldn't come, but hoped that I would except this present. It was
signed: "Your Pal, Mickey." It's easy to fix things when you're eight,
and I felt much better. Of course, I continued to invite Mickey to my
parties for a lot of years. And you know what? I really think he's
going to show up this year.

The End

44. Heartache

Thanks for coming over. I really need to talk to someone. *(Pause)* OK, how do I say this? *(Pause)* Tracy called last night and broke up with me. Wow, that's the first time I said it out loud. Don't worry, I'm OK I guess I'm just not sure how to deal with this. I know it's not the first time I've ever broken up with anybody, but it sure feels like it. You know what my first reaction was? I took that coffee mug with her name on it, it was one of her birthday gifts, and I went outside and threw it against a tree. *(Pause)* Well, it felt good at the time. Then I just sat and thought about the phone call. How she said that she just couldn't commit and that she loved me, but wasn't in love with me. God, I hate that line. She told me I was never anything but wonderful to her and she didn't know why things had changed, but they had. I knew that she was drifting away. That seemed to start right after she got back from vacation. The thing is, I saw it coming but I couldn't do anything about it. It gives you that real helpless feeling, you know what I mean? Anyway a lot of the call was the perfunctory garbage that is always said, but then she said she would call me in a couple of days and I heard myself say, "Why?" What is she going to say? I told her please don't call if you're going to give me that "I still want to be friends" speech. I don't want to be her pal. I don't need another drinking buddy. All she could say after that was, "Good-bye," and she hung up crying. Then the good part started. I tried to go to sleep. I laid in bed and I swear I could remember everything from the time we met till the phone call. I remembered in detail seeing her for the first time and watching her cross the room. She watched me too, but she wouldn't admit it till later. I remember our first kiss, which came before our first date. Do you know the only time we went away together she got sick, and I spent most of the time taking her temperature and holding her while she slept? Believe it or not it was a great trip. There was the time we went to the art museum and got yelled at for almost walking on an art piece we both thought was a part of the floor. Then there was our only New Year's and

1   Valentine's Day together. I'm mostly sorry I won't be able to share
2   all the things with her I wanted to. It's only been twelve hours since
3   she called and already I miss her. I keep seeing her smile and
4   hearing her laugh. Do you realize how big your bed can get in one
5   night? Who am I going to hold? Why did God give people emotions
6   and feelings? I wish I had an alarm that would go off when I was
7   starting to fall in love. I could avoid so much. *(He cries.)*
8   **The End**
9
10
11
12
13
14
15
16
17
18
19
20
21
22
23
24
25
26
27
28
29
30
31
32
33
34
35

45. Dating

GWEN: Men really tick me off. Not the whole species, mind you. Just a select group.

(Pause) The ones I date. And before you say it's because I'm bitter and can't get a date, it's actually the opposite. I have too many! Now, most people would say that having a lot of dates would be a good thing, but at this stage in my dating career I've come to realize that the number of men that I go out with is in direct correlation with the number of mistakes that I've made. See, if I could find one guy whose reality actually matched his original, initial potential, I wouldn't be dating the Who's-Who of non-commitment that I am. Want an example? OK, the doctor. *(Pause)* What a jerk! And why do I say that? Primarily because on his list of qualities, narcissism was number one. It never ceased to amaze me that a man with that amount of higher education only learned the meaning of the pronoun "I." I truly believe that if he ever used "you" it would have likely provoked permanent, irrevocable, cerebral damage. Following him was the affected, pretentious wine taster. That was a very short-lived affair. It actually may have worked out if I hadn't laughed in his face while he was trying to teach me how to taste wine and spit a delightful deep Burgundy all over his two-hundred-dollar silk shirt. Now, in all fairness there was one male that I really loved and got along with great. He was warm, he was kind, he was strong, he was loving — he was a German shepherd. Unfortunately he also belonged to a dweeb of a banker I was dating. That relationship lasted five months longer than it should have because I didn't want to give up the dog. From that guy, I went worldwide and got involved with an international banker. He was German *(Pause)* and gorgeous. *Ein was für Kerl!* God, he was gorgeous. When we first went out he spoke to me in German. Now, I'm not very fluent in German, so I took it upon myself to translate what he was saying to mean, "I love." So we did it. And things were going along great until he was called back to Germany and I never heard from him again. I think his company

1   was afraid that he was revealing international banking secrets or he
2   was abducted by the S.S. Either way, it was over.
3   Now recently, all these experiences got me thinking. There's got
4   to be a better way to find someone. Half the time I feel like I'm
5   shopping. Which in itself wouldn't be so bad except that when you
6   shop, something may look real good in the store, but when you
7   finally get it, it turns out that it doesn't always go with everything
8   you own. So I came up with a plan. Looking for a guy should be like
9   renting a video. You could go into a store and there they would all
10   be. All divided up into categories and sections for easy access and
11   perusal. Funny guys in the comedy section, serious in the drama.
12   The older and more distinguished would be in classics, and foreign
13   would be in ... well, the foreign section. The only problem I see
14   would be that the best-looking guys would probably be in the gay
15   section, which means "look but don't touch." Then, when you've
16   made your choice, you can check out the guy, view him at home, as
17   it were, and then decide if you want him to become a part of your
18   collection. There could even be weekend and midweek specials.
19   There would be a section to avoid: the previously viewed section.
20   The selections may look great, but inevitably, there's usually
21   something wrong with them. Also, one should try to avoid renting a
22   selection that someone else has suggested, unless you know of it
23   ahead of time.
24   This is the best solution to dating that I can think of. So ... what
25   do you think?

26   The End

27
28
29
30
31
32
33
34
35

46. The Fifties I

It's not easy being a girl nowadays. I have so many problems you wouldn't believe it. First off is my name. It's Julie. Now, don't get me wrong, it's a perfectly good name, but it's just not hip. I mean, Buddy Holly never wrote a song called "Julie." It's always Peggy Sue or Betty Lou or something like that. My middle name is Mildred. Somehow I don't think a song like Julie Mildred would sell. Do you? I have this friend named Barbara Ann and her boyfriend, this beach guy, wrote a song for her, but I don't think it will catch on.

Secondly, I'm having the hardest time figuring out an image. It took me six months to cultivate the Sandra Dee look. I got my hair in a ponytail just right, I learned to surf, I even got the kids to start calling me Gidget, and then guess what? Natalie Wood made a big hit in *Rebel without a Cause* and everyone started dying their hair dark and hanging out at drag races. So, I dyed my hair, started wearing scarves and bingo, Tuesday Weld got big. I was afraid to dye my hair again. I thought it might fall out so I let it grow out, but by the time it did, I missed the Tuesday Weld era. Isn't life a bitch?

And finally there's boys. All of them are so worried about being cool. I thought I spent a lot of time if front of the mirror. My boyfriend Tony spends so much time fixing his DA that we never go anywhere. And if we ever do go out, we meet up with all his friends and it's like being at a Marlon Brando convention.

So what I've finally decided is to wait for the Sixties to get here. I'm sure everyone will get back to normal by then. I mean, how much weirder can kids get?

The End

47. New Year's Eve

A little less than two hours ago we passed into a new year and already I've learned something new: You can't run away from a memory. Now at the outset this may appear to be an overly dramatic statement, but after one bottle of champagne and a good dose of self-indulgent self-pity, it's actually a very calm realization. Now, what brought this on? I'm very glad you asked. New Year's has always been a good or bad holiday. It all depends on whom I was with at the time. Tonight, I was alone, which means it already started out in the debit column. Anyway, I decided to go to this party that I was invited to, so I could get out of the house and be with other people. See, over the last couple of days I've started thinking about her. I don't know why, but I did. So I figured I'd go to this party and she wouldn't enter my mind. Yeah, right. Now, I'm sitting amongst about three or four hundred people and all that's going through my mind is New Year's Eve, three years ago. Want to guess who I was with? You got it. Her. Now midnight comes and I can hear her voice. I can see her eyes, and what's worse is that I can see that smile. That was the thing that always got to me. She had this smile that could light up my heart and make me feel like someone had stolen my knees. Now, one would think that since we had broken up almost three years ago that these feelings would have abated completely by now, wouldn't one? Logic dictates that, but when it comes to matters of the heart, logic rarely enters the picture and two plus two almost always equals five. So I started thinking, what was it about her? Was she, by definition, the sexiest woman I ever dated? No. Was she the most mature? No. Was she the most together? No. What she was, was one of the best persons I've ever met. Which in turn makes her the sexiest, most mature, most together, and any other adjective you might use. She made me … comfortable and feel good about myself and us. That may not seem like a lot, but it's everything in the world to me. Not a lot of women have made me feel that way. If they did, I'd never get any sleep because I'd be up at three o'clock every morning writing about them. I used to look forward to holding her hand, walking with her, talking with her, hugging her and never letting go. Unfortunately, she did let go. There are times when I miss her so damn much. Not all the time, not even a lot of the time, just ... sometimes. See, when something was truly good, no matter how long it lasted, a piece of these feeling will lock itself away in your soul forever for you to use and remember at your discretion. Since her, I've met a lot of women, dated some, made love to a few, but none yet have given me the same feeling when I've held them or made me as happy when I've woken up next to them. Though I'm pretty sure she doesn't think about me in the same way, I am sure I left her with something that, when she's alone, she'll remember and smile. How do I know this? Because no matter how hard you try, you can't run away from a memory. Happy New Year.

The End

48. The Fifties II

You know the other day my friend Tony said, "Yo, Joey, what do you think was the best decade to live in?" This struck me as a strange question from a guy who just got out of jail. So I answered him. I told him I thought the Fifties. He asked, "Why?" I said because they came after the Forties and before the Sixties. He said, "Thank you, Mr. Rocket Scientist." But, he didn't understand. See, the Forties was a strange time. I'm not sure you know, but there was a war going on then. My old man called it The Big One. W-W Two. I never did find out what W-W meant, but I guess it was the second whatever. Anyway, my old man said the war built men. He often told me, "You bum, you should have fought instead of staying home." I said, "Pop, I was only three in nineteen forty-four, what was I going to do? Lie to the draft? Tell 'em I was six?" So he smacked me in the head and said to stop being a smart aleck. Now, the Sixties — they were a weird time. I'm not sure you know, but there was a war going on then. My dad didn't even understand this one. I tried to tell him that it was a socio-economic police action. Sounds surprising coming out of me, huh? He smacked me in the head and told me not to be a smart aleck. Now, that leaves the Fifties. I was told there was a war there too, but I can't get anyone to confirm it. All I know is I was a teenager then, and a lot of important things happened. There was the DA, which gave birth to breakthroughs in hair grease. There was drag racing, which gave birth to the auto club. There was the Mickey Mouse Club and Annette, which gave birth to fantasies with ears. And there was the drive in, which gave birth to ... uh ... births. Now, people talk about all the things that were discovered since the start of time, but if you ask me, the Fifties gave us the best of all ... *Rock and Roll.*

The End

49. After a Year

I just realized that it's been a year since we broke up and I still miss him. The thing that's strange about it is, we only went out for six months. I told that to a friend of mine and he said that it seems to him that my sense of proportion was all screwed up. *(Pause)* I don't agree. See, I've only been in love twice in my life. Once, right before I left college, and him. I think that when it comes to love, time elements don't figure into it. Well, maybe for some people it does, but not for me, because after all this time I still hurt when I think about him. Now don't get me wrong. I don't mean it to sound like I go to bed crying every night or I'm planning to cut off my right ear *(Pause)* — or is it left? *(Pause)* Whatever — and send it to him. I just mean when I'm alone and it's quiet, thoughts of his eyes, his laugh … his touch. But — it's his smile that seems to wander through my mind and play with my emotions. You know, every time that happens I seem to remember the same three incidents. They weren't big, and I don't know why I think of them, but I do. Once was when we were asleep and I must've had a bad dream or something. I bolted awake and I remember him rubbing my back, saying, "It's OK, honey. It was only a dream." He rubbed my back till I fell asleep. The second is when he was away and he called and woke me up. He said that he was having a problem. I asked him what it was and he said that he missed me too much. The third one was very simple. We were sitting together watching a movie. I don't remember what it was, but we were just sitting there holding hands and … he just leaned over and kissed me on the cheek and sat back. I turned and looked at him and he smiled at me. That was it. He just smiled, but it gave me a warm feeling that … I just can't describe, but poets have made a fortune writing about it. It's the kind of feeling that if you ever felt it … well, you know. Anyway, what all this has made me realize is, when you have truly loved someone … a piece of you always will. No matter what the outcome. And you know what? *(Pause)* That's OK.

The End

50. The Rock Star

I called this press conference because I feel it's about time I cleared some things up. Before any of you ask, I got started about five years ago with some friends, fooling around in my garage. As far as my "meteoric rise to stardom" is concerned, I got lucky. Everyone always thinks that it takes years and years. Well, I've got news for you. It doesn't always. Sure, that's the usual way, but there are those cases where you were playing in the right place at the right time and you impressed the right person. That's what happened with me and my band. Anyway, I've been hearing a lot of bad about my band and I want to put a stop to it. I don't know where it's written that if you play Rock and Roll you have to be a drug addict or a slime bucket. I know that in the Sixties there was a lot of drug use, but that was then. It's not so much the case now. You know, I'll make a bet that if you look at all those people in our country who are lawyers, you'll find some drugs there too. This really goes for any profession you check into.

As to being a slime bucket, well sometimes we are, but we're only human. You know, I have been linked with everyone in the world. Do you know that last week I was having lunch in Paris with a princess, dinner in Rome with a Hollywood star, and believe it or not, on a tour of China with the band, all at the same time? This was according to one of the more reputable tabloids. The truth is, I was home last week with my wife and if she even thought I was doing any of those things, she promised to remove several anatomical parts of my body very painfully. So enough of that.

Now, I'd like to make just one last point. This is to the parents. I know that most of you don't like our music. OK, I don't mind that. Everyone has the right to their opinions, but don't put us down till you listen. You say that we are dangerous, well that's not true. I've listened to some old music where the singers said to, "Beat me Daddy, eight to the bar." This sounds a little masochistic to me, but I never said it should be banned. To each his own. I think all I've wanted to say all along was that we really are good people. Just give

1 us a chance. Oh, by the way, if you still think I'm dangerous, it
2 might make you feel better if you all know that my real name is
3 Marvin Schwartz. How dangerous can I be? Rock on.
4   **The End**
5
6
7
8
9
10
11
12
13
14
15
16
17
18
19
20
21
22
23
24
25
26
27
28
29
30
31
32
33
34
35